MODULAR PROGRAMMING

MODULAR PROGRAMMING

JEFF MAYNARD, L.B.C.S.

First Edition

petrocelli
books

New York, 1972

© Butterworth & Co (Publishers) Ltd, 1972

First US edition published in 1972
Second printing by Petrocelli Books, a division of
Mason & Lipscomb, N.Y., September 1973

Internationnal Standard Book Number: 0—88405—018—1
Library of Congress Catalog Card Number: 75—187890

Library of Congress Cataloging in Publication Data

Maynard, Jeff.
Modular programming.

1.   Modular programming.   I.   Title.
QA76.6M395   1973   001.6'424   73—19921
ISBN 0—88405—018—1

Printed in Great Britain

PREFACE

My interest in methods designed to reduce the development costs involved in programming and to minimise the tedium sometimes involved therein goes back to my early days in computing. This time was spent programming for a KDF6 machine and was, I consider, a marvellous introduction to computing. Although a large amount of program design time was spent attempting to accommodate the program in 4 K words of storage it was obvious then that a great deal of effort was wasted by duplication of coding already done elsewhere and it was equally obvious that the complete testing of one-piece programs was virtually impossible. Unfortunately, the hardware and the software available was not suited to alternative methods.

It was not until a few years later that I was able to pursue my embryonic ideas with the aid of System 360 architecture and software. In fact the methods of program design, structure and testing discussed in this book are made possible by the structure of third generation computers. A large amount of practical research into modular programming indicated to me that whilst software testing and linking is essential to the mechanics of the method, the full benefits will only be realised if the program design stage is correctly undertaken. Accordingly, this text discusses the modular design of programs in some detail before explaining the workings of the method.

This book is primarily written to enable programming managers and programmers to comprehend and then implement modular programming for their own work. More senior management with some data processing involvement will get an appreciation of the potential benefits of modular programming by reading Chapter 1 and Chapter 2 and those with some knowledge of computers will learn the principles of it by reading Chapters 1–9.

I would like to thank Paul Marriotti with whom I had some interesting discussions prior to producing my final manuscript.

J.M.

CONTENTS

One

TRADITIONAL METHODS

Many programming departments have a very poor success rating within their Company because of their consistent failure to meet specified deadlines. (Even assuming a deadline is met does not of course mean that the programs will function 100 per cent correctly.) Many reasons are put forward for the failure of programming departments — lack of effective scheduling, inconsistent or ambiguous specifications, inadequate training facilities, mis-management, and so on. Whilst undoubtedly some of these reasons will be true in many cases, it is also true that the faults of many programming departments do not fall into any of these categories and, even where they do, the fault given is only superficial and does not reflect the true reason for the short-comings of the department. The failing then is clearly at a more fundamental level — but what is it? Is the choice of programming language wrong? Are the standards unenforceable or unworkable? Is the Software Support inadequate or inefficient? The answer to all these questions is NO.

   The fault in fact undermines the very foundation of the department since it is in such a fundamental area. This being the method used to write the program. This does not mean the choice of language but refers to the 'building' method used to produce the program from nothing. When programming was in its infancy the coding for a pro-gram would be started from the beginning of the specification and continued through instruction-by-instruction until the complete program was coded. Only then would testing begin. On some of the older machines with perhaps only 4 K of storage this traditional method was not too bad a compromise with better but more time consuming testing methods. It is alarming to note that many third generation installations are still using traditional methods of designing program structures. However, it is not now uncommon to find partition sizes of 30—60 K and to attempt to fill this in one piece will almost certainly lead to trouble. The programmer who has used only the traditional methods of program design will immediately attack the previous statement and demand to know what is meant by trouble when he has been programming without trouble for many years. This is not an unusual reaction since the problems with traditional programming methods can often remain hidden and only manifest themselves in the overall reduction of departmental throughput.

This book is obviously going to put forward alternative methods of designing programs but before that is done it will be useful to examine in detail the problems referred to above.

THE PROBLEMS OF TRADITIONAL OR MONOLITHIC PROGRAMMING

The difficulties outlined below are given in some cases merely as statements rather than detailed explanations: anyone who has worked in a commercial programming department will readily appreciate these points, but for the benefit of non-programmers it should be pointed out that the author's comments are based on seven years' commerical programming experience not only in a wide cross-section of industry, but also for a leading Software House.

Progress Reporting

The successful management of any production (including the production of computer programs) relies upon accurate and timely progress reporting and the interpretation of this reporting as it relates to the schedules for the work involved. The ideal situation is to reduce the departmental load to a number of small units of work such that progress reporting need only consist of an indication that a particular unit is either started or complete. If, for example, each unit of work is expected to require two man-days' effort progress reporting can at most be wrong by two days. It will not be necessary to report progress within each unit of work.

However, in monolithic programming it is very difficult to produce reporting points other than

CHART
CODE
PUNCH
CLEAN LIST
TEST

The final unit in this list (TEST) may involve anything up to three months effort and during this period it is almost impossible to determine accurately whether or not testing is on time. How many times has a program been 95 per cent working or 'almost finished' for six or seven weeks?

Even if a program appears to be working as the completion date draws near it is quite possible for a small undiscovered flaw to suddenly set back the testing by an unacceptable amount.

Fragility

The complete testing of monolithic programs is virtually impossible due to the very large number of total logic paths. However, it is usually possible to test all the main logic early in the program test stage; nevertheless it is not unknown for major logic errors to be discovered during System Testing. For example, the final testing of a file-match program may produce a complicated trailer record situation which the program is unable to handle due to a lack of record stacking areas and the required logic. No time would be available to rewrite the program to cater for this situation so instead hurried corrections or patches would be dropped in. The program would now work but only in rather a 'botched up' manner — it would in fact be 'fragile' in that its logic would be very difficult to amend at a later stage in development.

Staffing

Programmers tend very much to be individualists and they like to demonstrate this in their programs. This is particularly true where low-level or assembly languages are in use when the programmer will devise a great many abstruse methods of coding simple routines purely to keep his mind active when involved in a long coding job. The first problem with this is encountered when the program author starts to test his work since he often cannot remember how he intended a particular section of coding to work. A far more serious problem arises if the original author decides to leave (or is away ill) before testing of the program is completed. Before a replacement can complete the testing he has not only to find out the functions of the program and the amount of testing already complete, but he must also discover all the unusual or non-standard coding techniques that the author used when originally writing the program. When a programmer leaves during testing it is clear that a significant delay will be incurred to that program's schedule either because another programmer will need to become familiar with it or in the worst case by having to rewrite the entire program.

Machine Time for Testing

Programmers do not in general like to test the programs out of office hours or wait two or three days for a test-shot to be returned and yet most commercial installations have very little free time available during the prime shift. Even with modern compilers a large program may take up to 15 min to compile and test (particularly if large test files are involved), and finding this amount of machine time between production runs can be very difficult.

Balance of Workload

A particular program may require a small section of complicated coding, such as address calculation for a direct access file, which can only be written by an experienced programmer in assembly language. To have this programmer write the entire program purely because of this one routine is wasteful of effort particularly if the remainder of the program is relatively simple.

Similarly it is difficult to find work for junior and trainee programmers since they can only be given specifications for programs that are simple throughout (e.g. print programs). Not only can these two factors cause dissatisfaction but they can also lead to a situation where some programmers are overloaded with work whilst others have very little to do. To obtain the best from any department it is clearly necessary to ensure as much as possible that everybody has a constant load of the right type of work.

Re-invention of the Wheel

In a commercial programming department a number of programs will always be similar, e.g. there will always be a number of cardedit

4

programs, and therefore certain sections of coding within one of these programs will be similar or even identical to a section within another program. Writing in monolithic style these similar pieces of coding will be rewritten and retested by different programmers as each separate program is developed. Clearly this duplication of effort is very time wasting and extremely costly.

Scheduling

Estimating the amount of effort involved in the development of a large monolithic program is very difficult, if not impossible. Unless the forward work load is known it is impossible to produce accurate schedules or realistic deadlines as well as being difficult to determine manpower and machine time requirements.

From what has been said above it is clear that traditional or monolithic programming methods are unsatisfactory both for programmer motivation and for departmental efficiency. The solution to some or all of these problems would seem to be a reduction in the size of the programs under development. However, not only would this not be very successful (since we would still be dealing with relatively large chunks of complicated logic), but it would also mean that the programming department's capabilities are placing constraints on systems design. However, a solution is available that involves very small manageable units of work which themselves form only part of a large complex program.

Two

MODULAR PROGRAMMING — AN INTRODUCTION

In order that the throughput of a programming department can be improved, it is necessary to reduce the units of work to small manageable segments such that each of these segments can be scheduled and developed as an independent unit. Writing programs in this way is the theory behind Modular Programming and an extract from the Glossary defines it thus:

'Modular programming is a system of developing programs as a set of interrelated individual units (called modules) which can later be linked together to form a complete program'. It is not sufficient, however, merely to think in terms of subroutines or 'a page of the specification equals a module' since an approach like this can lead to an increase in the development times of programs because the splitting into modules has been made on a haphazard basis. For modular programming to be successful within an installation it must be implemented within a proven framework that has the understanding and agreement of the personnel to whom it is directed.

The splitting of program specifications into modules becomes perhaps the most important function within a department and it is quite common to find Senior Programmers devoting the majority of their working week to program design. At first sight this may seem to be a backward step since it removes from the programming load the most experienced staff. However, this is not the case since most modules will be easy to program, and do not therefore require very experienced staff, and the overall development time saved will easily outweigh any time 'lost' by having Senior Programmers doing program design.

The production of individual modules from a program specification is discussed in detail later in the book, but it can be said here that it is based on the logical functions required by a program. Each module will therefore perform a single logical function (e.g. Read Input File) or a number of small related logical functions (e.g. Gross to Nett computation). Once these logical functions have been isolated each module

6

can be coded and tested on its own and only when all the modules of a program are written and tested need they all be linked together for final program testing.

Modular programming relies on the relocatability and linkage edit (compose) features of third generation machines in order to function. Any reader not familiar with these terms or with the use of Linkage Sections, DSECT'S, CALL statements or parameter lists is recommended to read the relevant parts of the Glossary and the final chapter of this book before continuing.

ADVANTAGES OF MODULAR PROGRAMMING

Modular programming is not a panacea of programming ills, it will not cure the D.P. Manager's ulcer overnight nor will it dispense with the need for standards, training procedures and well-motivated programmers. Modular programming can, however, when successfully implemented within an installation, cause a significant improvement in the development of new programs and can improve in particular the areas of program quality, departmental flexibility, standardisation, scheduling, control and maintenance and machine utilisation.

Program Quality

An average program specification is usually too large to be fully understood at one time, particularly when it is first passed to the programming department. What this means is that there is too much logic within that program for a programmer to form a complete mental picture of what is required. When this is the case it is not possible for the programmer to effectively eliminate redundant code nor is it possible for him to readily see that the logic he intends using is correct. Additionally, there is the danger that the programmer will introduce logic errors or that he will misinterpret the intentions of the specification writer. A module which has been defined according to the methods described later (i.e. performs a single logical function or small group of interrelated logical functions) can be readily comprehended and a complete mental picture of its logic can be formed. This has the double advantage of ensuring that greater attention is paid to the detailed logic of each piece of coding and that very few, if any, logic errors are written into the module.

Since each module is small logically, and probably small instruction-wise, it is easy for the programming manager to ensure that the installation coding standards are being adhered to and that full and accurate documentation is being maintained. Furthermore, this verification can be carried out on a spot check basis since any given module can be examined in detail in a very short time. Each unit of coding is therefore of high quality, will conform to installation standards and, as will be shown later, is better tested. The program produced by linking the modules together will itself be also of high quality.

Flexibility

Modular programming permits greater freedom in the choice of programming language and in the allocation of staff to a particular project. It is no longer necessary to assign an experienced programmer to a program simply because it contains one difficult piece of coding. The experienced programmer can still be used to write the difficult section of coding but the remaining simple modules can, if required, be given to other members of the department. It is even possible to give a simple module to a trainee programmer immediately he returns from his first course; not only will this make him productive earlier, but it will also give him a feeling of responsibility and usefulness.

The elapsed development time for a program can, when required, be considerably reduced by having a number of programmers develop individual modules from the program in parallel.

Standardisation

Two different meanings can be attached to standardisation when considered as an advantage of modular programming.

Adherence to the Installation Standards Manual is difficult to enforce with monolithic programming because it requires the Programming Manager or Chief Programmer to spend a considerable amount of time investigating the methods used in any given program and to examine its documentation. However, as previously mentioned, a module, being small, can easily be completely looked over as can its documentation.

When writing a suite of programs certain functions will invariably occur in more than one program. It is extremely uneconomic to recode

8

the function in each program, however, if the function is in a self-contained module it need only be written and tested once. Once modular programming is introduced a great many standard modules soon become available and a library made up of these can save a considerable amount of duplication of effort.

Scheduling

Estimating accurately the amount of effort involved in coding a large program is very difficult and is usually based on guesswork. Without knowing exactly how much work is involved it is impossible to produce accurate schedules and difficult to assess whether or not existing man-power is sufficient to meet any required deadlines. When scheduling modular programs, however, the unit of work involved is small enough to be fully comprehensive and it becomes practical therefore to estimate accurately how much work is involved in developing a given module. Once the effort has been determined for each module the total effort required to produce the program is available.

The scheduled time for any given module will be quite small — generally two elapsed weeks or less with a loading of 5 modules, i.e. 2 man-days effort per module — therefore accurate and meaningful progress returns are soon available and re-scheduling can be carried out if necessary. Since the total effort involved in a module is small it is no longer necessary to receive intermediate progress returns but only to know that it has been started and then that it has been completed.

In the worst case when a module is scrapped and has to be rewritten only a very small effort is required and the overall program deadline is unlikely to be affected.

Control and Maintenance

Programming departments tend to have a high rate of staff turnover which can introduce severe setbacks into a development schedule if a programmer leaves part way through the testing stage of a large program. This problem is virtually eliminated with modular programming since it is a relatively easy task to reschedule modules not yet started and modules under development are easily taken over by another member of the department. As mentioned above a module that requires rewriting will not have a very disastrous effect upon the overall project schedule. Machine time usage for program development is much easier to control for three reasons:

(1) Because the amount of coding effort involved in a module is accurately known it is feasible to estimate accurately the number of test shots that will be required to test that module. Most modules will require a similar number of test shots and if some form of machine time usage reporting system is in use, it will be possible to identify excessive use of testing time by any particular programmer.

(2) During the later stages of program development when groups of modules are being tested together it is only necessary to recompile or reassemble those modules that have had coding changes since the previous test. Excessive machine time will not therefore be wasted by constant recompilation of working code.

(3) The amount of machine time required to compile and test a single module may be in the order of 1—2 min. It is obviously easier therefore to slot in odd test-shots during production running.

The maintenance of production programs is always a problem because no one in the department likes doing it and because it requires a lot of time to be spent finding out the area of the program to be altered. Having altered the relevant section of coding it is then necessary to checkout the entire program thoroughly. However, if the program was written in a modular fashion it will usually be a simple task to isolate the one or two modules requiring amendment. These modules can easily be amended (or even rewritten) and thoroughly tested without any amendment to the production program. Only when the amendment is fully checked-out in the module need the program be relinked and itself tested simply (only the module linkages should need testing in this case).

Machine Utilisation

As already mentioned modular programming can reduce the testing time requirements and thereby improve machine utilisation. However, it can further improve this utilisation in other ways. An alteration in method of operating may require that the partition sizes be reduced (to introduce multi-programming for example), but to suddenly be required to overlay a monolithic program can be a difficult if not impossible task. However, as will be described in detail later, to overlay a modularised program is quite easy and can often be accomplished merely by amending the link-edit (compose) job control card set-up.

When multi-programming is in use it may be required to have the option of selecting direct or 'spool' printing at run time. To incorporate this facility into a previously written modularised program is again an easy task.

Three

MODULARISING

Before a program can be written in modules a certain amount of program design must be carried out. It is not sufficient to give a program specification to a programmer with the comment 'write this in a modular fashion', and expect him to complete the job in record time. Although modular programming is only an aid to program development it is essential that it be approached in a defined manner if the full benefits are to be realised.

PROGRAM DESIGN

The stage in program development immediately prior to coding becomes the most critical function to be tackled during this development. If the design of the program structure is incorrect the final testing stage may well prove to be such a stumbling block that development has to be set back an unacceptable amount. The main output requirement of the program design or modularisation stage is a module linkage chart and a number of module specifications.

The module linkage chart (Figure 3.1) will show each module in the program with its hierarchical position and its relationships with the other modules. This chart shows a program structured with three levels of module. Module A can call modules B, C and D and module D can call module E. Any inter-module calls must only be downwards and along an unbroken line, i.e. module A cannot call module E directly but only via module D. Module B cannot call module C since this would require a sideways call — in order for this calling sequence to be valid the chart would need to be redrawn as in Figure 3.2. Now it can be seen that, if required, module D can be allowed to call module C although module C cannot now gain access to module E. It is important to stress the difference between actual lines of module communication and additional permitted lines. In Figure 3.2 module D is not linked

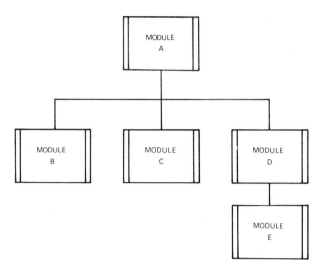

Figure 3.1

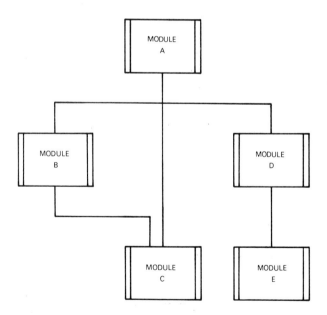

Figure 3.2

with module C and will not therefore call it in the program. However, since module C is at a lower level than module D it would be permissible to add a communication line between these two modules (Figure 3.3).

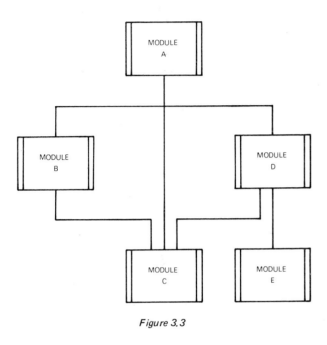

Figure 3.3

Similarly module B could be linked with module E although not with module D.

Return Paths

As calling sequences can only be downward along unbroken lines so return paths must not only be upwards along unbroken lines but must also be the exact reverse of the calling path. In the above example if the calling sequence is module A-module D-module C, then the return to module A from module C must be made via module D. (Even if module D has no further processing to do before returning to module A.)

14

Although it is a relatively easy task to amend the coding of module C to return directly to module A it is most important that this is not done for two reasons:

(1) As soon as the linkages of module C are tampered with it becomes impossible to slot in another module between say modules D and C or between modules A and C without amending module C.

(2) The standard method of linkage has been abandoned and therefore module C (and possibly module D) is peculiar to this program and cannot therefore be used, unaltered, in the development of a later program.

Types of Module

Module A in Figure 3.3 is called a CONTROL module since its function is to control the calling sequence of the lower level modules and to communicate with the operating system. The control module will normally do no processing other than that required to determine the calling sequence of the lower levels and to introduce any overlay phases into core. There are, however, two exceptions to these rules — when some complicated logic is required to determine a calling sequence this may be done in a lower level module which passes back an indicator to the control module and the control module may contain any odd sections of coding which do not conveniently fit into another module (or are too trivial to justify a separate module).

The other (lower level) modules in the diagram can be of two types:

(1) PROCESS modules are those which form the 'heart' of the program since they perform the basic processing of the program. Each process module will perform a single logical function or a series of small related logical functions. During their processing process modules may call other process modules or input/output modules (see below). At the logical end of a process module is a return point (q.v.) which will transfer control back to the calling module (q.v.) at a point immediately following the point of invocation (q.v.) within the calling module.

(2) INPUT/OUTPUT modules perform an I/O function for a single file including automatic opening of the file on the first call (this is to

avoid special 'opening' calls which may not be present when testing
a small subset of the module linkage chart as a single module).

I/O modules will do no processing other than to set an indicator when
End of File is reached or to test an indicator that requests for a file to be
closed. A module which read a single card (a date card for example)
and validated it as conforming to the installation standards would be
classed as a process module not an I/O module.

THE SEVEN STAGES

In order that the developed program is modularised in the best possible
manner and therefore is developed in the shortest possible time, it is
necessary to produce more than just a module linkage chart and module
specifications. It is essential that some thought be given to such things
as programming languages and need of overlays before coding commences. In other words these and other areas must be examined at the
modularisation stage.
   In order that this is achieved the specification must be examined
not only from the point of view of breaking into logical functions but
in a number of other areas giving altogether the following seven stages
of modularisation.

(1) The Initial Breakdown
(2) Use of Standard Modules
(3) Definition of Interfaces
(4) Choice of Programming Language
(5) Selection of Staff
(6) Usage of Core Storage
(7) Testing Requirements

Once a programmer has some experience of modularising program
specifications he will probably cover all seven aspects at one time as he
breaks down the specification. However, it is useful when first using
the techniques described in this book to attempt each stage as a
separate exercise; in this way a full appreciation of the need for each
of the stages will be acquired. To illustrate the seven stages in the
following chapters the sample program specified below is used. The
reader should familiarise himself with this program before proceeding.

Program 'Sample'
Specified By A. N. Analyst

Set Up

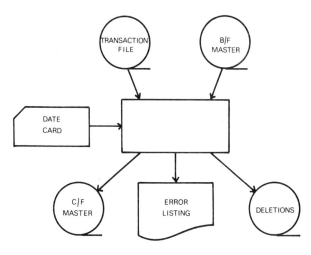

Figure 3.4

Files

TRANSACTIONS	contains this week's transactions sorted out by code (1 add, 2 update, 3 delete) within customer key. Final record (Code 9, customer key all '9') has count of all code types on file
B/F MASTER	contains one record for each current customer showing name/address, current balance and various status information
C/F MASTER	as B/F
DELETIONS	contains one record for each customer deleted this week with a non-zero balance outstanding
DATE CARD	Card type D20 contains program run date and month-end indicator
ERROR LISTING	one line for each rejected transaction and one line for each month-end negative balance outstanding

Throughput   The date card is read and stored for later use.
Transaction file is read and matched against the
B/F master file. A type 1 (ADD) transaction matching with the B/F master is rejected and an error
report produced, otherwise a new master file
record is created and written to the C/F master.
Transaction type 2 and 3 matching with the B/F
master are used to update or delete the master
file respectively. If a customer to be deleted
has a non-zero balance a record is written to the
deletions file.

When month end is indicated each customer
written to the B/F master produces an error
report if it has a negative balance outstanding.
Note that a record may be added, updated and
deleted in the same run.

At end of file the control totals should be
checked with the all 9 record and an error report
logged if an out-of-balance occurs. Any unmatched
transaction types 2 and 3 are rejected with an
error report.

If either input file is out of sequence the program
must be terminated with an appropriate error
logging.

Four

SPECIFICATIONS AND THE LINKAGE CHART

THE SPECIFICATION

Before the specification is broken down it is important that the
modulariser satisfies himself that the specification supplied is acceptable
to the programming department. The specification should be clear and
unambiguous and sufficiently detailed to permit the program to be
fully developed without further reference to the Systems Department.
The degree of detail in the specification will of course vary from
installation to installation since different people have different ideas
as to the level of detail required. However, it is important to agree with
the Systems Department that it is a system specification which is to be
provided and not a detailed program narrative. Many systems analysts,
especially those with a programming background, write program
specifications in such detail that they are almost a high-level language
procedure. This of course has the effect of turning programmers into
coders, with consequent problems. However, a further complication
can arise when modular programming is an installation standard:
systems analysts tend to write their specifications in sections
which they think should form the modules of the final program. This
is very bad practice since analysts are very rarely the best people to do
the modularisation because of: (1) their lack of contact with such
things as operating systems, and programming techniques and the
degree of module standardisation in use at the installation, and (2)
the fact that a specification already modularised will probably not
be checked for logic by the programming department. The fact that
modular programming techniques are used by the programmers should
make no difference to the way in which the analysts write specifications.

The Initial Breakdown

The first stage of modularisation is the production of an initial module
linkage chart showing the basic spilt into modules. The first step therefore

19

is to write down an initial FUNCTION LIST, i.e. a list of the basic logically separate parts of the program. No attempt is made at this stage to define an order of these functions and nor is any attempt made to derive functions all at the same level within the logical structure.

The function list for the specification in Chapter 3 could be written down thus:

(a) File handling
(b) File matching
(c) File end processing
(d) Customer record processing
(e) Error reporting
(f) Abort procedures

Having produced this function list we now have to decide which functions can be done in the control module. Bearing in mind the description of a control module given in the preceding chapter, we can allocate functions (b), (c) and (f).

Function (b) (file matching) is required to control the sequence of calling the lower level modules (see below) and is a fairly simple piece of logic (Figure 4.1). If the file matching logic was very complex it could be made into a process module which would return an indicator (equal, high, low) to the control module.

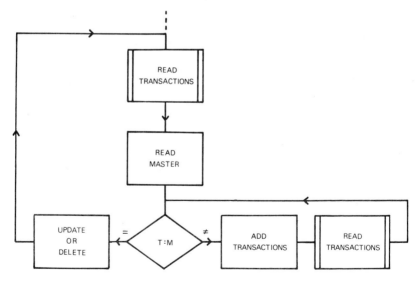

Figure 4.1

Function (c) is included in the control module because it is fairly straightforward. In this example the only end-of-file processing required is to check the control totals and close the files. (Note, however, that coding will need to be incorporated to cater for the case of a transaction file shorter than the master file or vice versa.) A program requiring complicated control total computations could have this processing performed in a separate end-of-file process module.

Function (f) is included in the control module because of its trivial nature. Each file will be checked for sequence with an operator message and forced end-of-job if an error is detected.

Module Linkage Chart

At each step in the initial breakdown a module linkage chart is produced. The modules or functions so far determined are as follows:

Control
File handling
Customer record processing
Error reporting

This will produce a linkage chart as in Figure 4.2. Each box (except control) must now be examined to determine if it contains more than

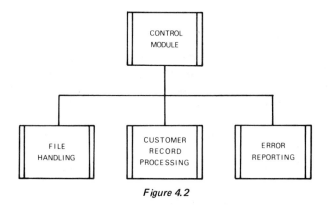

Figure 4.2

one distinct logical function and can therefore be split into further modules. The first obvious target is 'file handling' since the program handles four basic files (the print file is not yet considered since it is included in 'error reporting'). The handling of each file will now become a separate function producing a linkage chart as shown in Figure 4.3. (The reason for the first module being 'Read & *Validate*' will be discussed in the next chapter.)

The examination of each 'first level' box is continued until all have been dealt with. The 'customer record processing' can be seen to con-

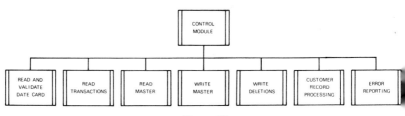

Figure 4.3

tain four separate functions — Addition, Updating, Deletion and Month End (*see* Figure 4.4), which can be split into four modules. A further examination to discover any more functions reveals that three modules (Month End, Add and Exceptions) produce printed output; a separate module will therefore be created to transmit print images to a printer (or, if required, to a print image tape).

The ADD module will produce a detailed print of the new record and a separate module will therefore be created to produce it. A record is written to the Deletions File only if a certain condition is specified during the DELETE module. Rather than retain an indicator to the control module indicating whether or not the deletions file module is required, it can be called directly from the DELETE module. The module linkage chart will now appear as in Figure 4.5. The examination of the module linkage chart and its expansion is continued until all the logical functions of the program have been isolated into *manageable* units. Obviously certain functions could be combined, e.g. Read and Write master file, but these would not necessarily prove manageable and would almost certainly not be usefully standard (*see* Chapter 5). Similarly, some modules could be split into smaller and smaller functions almost to the point where each module contained one instruction. Clearly this is an unlikely extreme, but care must be taken not to make modules much smaller than a 'manageable' size, because of the overheads introduced by modular programming (extra specifications, testing, linkages, etc., — *see* Chapter 13).

22

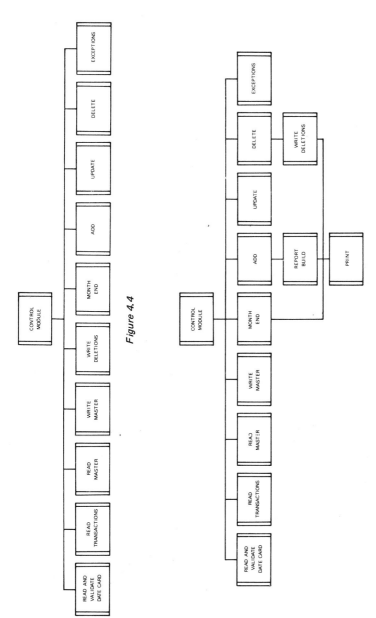

Figure 4.4

Figure 4.5

Five

STANDARD MODULES

One of the great advantages of modular programming is that it produces small sections of easily reusable coding. A single module can very simply be 'lifted' from an existing program and slotted into another. In some cases this would be done by physically duplicating the source deck cards of the module although most third generation operating systems permit the user to store object deck modules on the Systems Residence Device to be linked with other modules as desired. Clearly then if a module already exists for a function within a new program the effort required to link it in to the program is considerably less than the effort required to recode the module specially for the new program.

It would be very nice if all new programs could be written using already available modules from a library and involving therefore only the preparation of some job control cards and the writing of a control module. This may well come about but at present the idea represents only a Data Processing Manager's dream and a programmer's nightmare! Standard modules are not normally available for much in the way of processing or for unusual calculations since these functions are by their nature not very standard. A standard module can be described as one which performs a function which is known to be required in future programs or which has a high possibility of being usable in a future program or programs.

These two types of standard module tend to come into being in different manners. When a new installation is set up or when a new system is designed any experienced programmer will, after a brief look at the system proposals, be able to list a number of functions which will occur in more than one program. The most obvious of these is file handling since every commercial program will handle at least one file and almost every file will be operated upon by more than one program. Other functions which will fall into the same category as file-handling include:

    check digit generation/verification;
    date verification;
    page heading routines;
    account number range tests;
    name and address alphabetic tests.

Since these functions are known requirements it is usual, and indeed, desirable, to schedule their programming before any other work is started on the remainder of the suite of programs. In the case of a new installation it is very worthwhile to set up these standard routines before any other development work is commenced. Producing standard modules as a specific exercise not only has the advantage of reducing future programming effort but also enables more thought and more expertise to be applied to the coding involved. For example, file handling modules could be written to work in the Locate mode rather than the Move mode with a consequent saving in core storage space; check digit routines which often involve a considerable amount of arithmetical data handling, could be written in Assembly language with a consequent improvement in efficiency.

Modules to meet a known need are therefore produced, but also modules which may meet an expected need tend to evolve. The first step in Stage 2 of the modularisation process (Use of Standard Modules) is to discover what standard modules already exist for functions within the projected program. In the case study it could be expected that five modules would already be in existance (the four file handling routines and the print output routine). For these modules no specification is required since this will already exist in the Module Library documentation (see below) and no further work is therefore required at this stage.

It is important also to examine the linkage chart for signs of under-modularisation. In other words it is possible to specify a module containing several functions one or more of which already exist in a standard module. If this is the case the linkage chart should be redrawn to reflect the lower-level processing. The module specification will of course be less complicated since it involves fewer processing steps and the module itself when written, will require less testing.

The second step in this stage is to examine the remaining projected modules to see if any can be redesigned such that a useful standard module results. It should be noted that any module, once written, is obviously available for use later if the need for its precise function should arise. However, at this stage we are concerned only with reasonable expectations and should not therefore spend a great deal of time incorporating extra processing in modules on the off-chance that they will be useful later.

It is quite possible that when the module linkage chart is drawn a function will be identified that is obviously going to be required again in the future. (For example, a routine to convert the date in Julian form to the more usual collating form YYDDD.) This will particularly occur if the known requirements for standard modules have not been met as a specific exercise. We are also concerned at this stage with evaluating each module to discover if by the addition of a *small* amount of processing, it will become useful elsewhere and examining the module structure to see if a slight restructuring would produce one or more standard modules.

In the case study we have a combination of these lines of thought. The reading and validating of the date card could have expected to be done as in Figure 5.1. However, a single module (Read AND Validate Card)

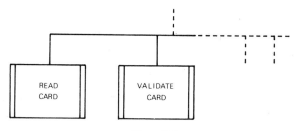

Figure 5.1

has been decided upon. This may seem, at first glance, to be a backward step! The reasons for doing this, however, are quite valid and indicate a piece of modularising that might easily escape all but the more experienced program designer. Only one program in this suite reads more than one card and it would be inefficient therefore to incorporate in all the other programs (which all require a date card) a module which contained coding to read cards double buffered and which contained two card input areas. If this module were written in assembly language it would not need any I/O areas since this could be supplied by the control module (use of a general work area would of course save even more core).

26

Often a module required in a current program will appear to be 'almost' useful elsewhere. In this case it is good practice to incorporate the extra processing (perhaps additional options) in the module when it is specified for this program. The extra work involved will almost certainly be less than that required later to either amend the current module or write a new one to perform the additional function. In the case study the month-end routine produces only a print-line; however, in another program the month-end procedure could also involve rolling up the previous 'n' weeks payment figures. Both functions can be incorporated in the one module with a simple indicator to request the additional processing.

MODULE LIBRARY

Modules are usually small amounts of coding representing only perhaps a few man-days effort. It does not take very long therefore for an installation to gather a large collection of tested modules. Of these some, as we have seen, will have become standard modules because of their potential use to others. However, they are only of use if the programmer working on a future project is aware of their existence. It is essential then to set up some form of module library to which easy reference can be made.

A module library must obviously contain the modules themselves but it must also contain a comprehensive and easily accessible index and descriptions. The modules in the library will be held normally in source and object form although the source decks will usually be for back-up purposes only. Programming departments must take full advantage of the linkage facilities offered by third generation operating systems to avoid the time wasted by recompilation or reassembly of working sections of coding. The source decks can therefore be held purely as physical card decks kept in fire-proof storage cabinets and should only be used in cases of emergency (i.e. when the systems residence has been corrupted and the back-up does not contain all the modules normally held in the library). Some operating systems provide a source language library and update facility which can be used as a first line back-up (card decks being the second-line back-up). Object language decks can also be held on punched cards although this should again only be for back-up purposes. Card decks which are in use daily soon become shabby and unreadable and may even be dropped and lose their sequence. The object modules should be held on a tape or disc library which is readily accessible by the system and which can easily be updated. Most operating systems now provide this feature although if they do not it is not a difficult task to write a library processor suite of programs to set-up and maintain such a library. Each module in the library must obviously be fully documented so that the programmer can determine if a module suits his requirements. To this end a manual should be available, either for a department or for each programmer, containing a detailed processing description, list of parameters and a flow chart. The format of module descriptions and module specifications is discussed in detail later in this book.

FINDING A MODULE

It is no use having a large comprehensive library with full documentation for each entry if programmers are unable to find out if the module they want is available. The longer an installation using modular programming progresses the more acute this problem will become if there is no formalised system. When a module library is first established it is quite in order to have a list of the modules available pinned to the department notice board; alternatively the programmers can read through the module descriptions. However, a point will be reached when the list becomes out of date or incomplete or the number of module descriptions is too large to be looked through frequently or memorised. If nothing is done at this stage a serious duplication of effort can occur as programmers code modules which are already available but of which they are not aware.

The solution to this problem is to have a list of all the modules available which gives a brief description of the function of each. To facilitate quick reference each entry in the list should contain no more than one line. It would also be useful if this list were arranged in a pre-determined order designed to speed up a search of it. Any library maintenance system will obviously include facilities for listing the current contents of the library, unfortunately this list will not suit the searching role because it will normally only contain the module name (usually limited to about eight characters) and version number and will be in the wrong order (usually the order the modules were catalogued to the library).

28

To overcome these problems it is easy enough to write a small suite of programs to provide a comprehensive catalogue list arranged in such a way that finding a desired module is quick and easy. The best method of presenting the list is probably by KeyWord-In-Context (KWIC) with one descriptive line or title for each module. If desired, each line can also contain status information such as date catalogued, version number, etc. In a KWIC index each entry may appear several times, one for each occurrence of a keyword or significant word (non-significant words are those such as: the, an, a, module, file, and can be chosen to suit the user). The small sample section of a KWIC index shown below will illustrate the general format and the ease with which a particular function can be identified or eliminated.

TITLE	NAME	VERSION
PAYCHECKS, SORT INTERNALLY	PAYSRT3	2
PRINT WEIGHBRIDGE TICKETS	VALTKSP	1
PURGE UPDATED ACCOUNT-RECS	ACUPPRG	4
RATE FILE, READ MASTER	STMRDMR	1
READ MASTER RATE FILE	STMRDMR	1
READ MASTER TRANS FILE	STMRDTF	1
RE-ORDER LEVELS, ROLL	ACUPROLL	3
ROLL RE-ORDER LEVELS	ACUPROLL	3
SORT PAYCHECKS INTERNALLY	PAYSRT3	2
TICKETS, WEIGHBRIDGE, PRINT	VALTKSP	1
TICKETS, WEIGHBRIDGE, VALIDATE	VALTKTSV	1
TRANS FILE READ MASTER	STMRDTF	1
UPDATE CHECK DIGIT	CHKDIGUP	1
UPDATE DAY-OF-WEEK CODE	DYWKUP	2
UPDATED ACCOUNT-RECS, PURGE	ACUPPRG	4
VALIDATE CARD-TYPE D20	VALCD20	1
VALIDATE WEIGHBRIDGE TICKETS	VALTKTSV	1
WEIGHBRIDGE TICKETS, PRINT	VALTKSP	1
WEIGHBRIDGE TICKETS, VALIDATE	VALTKTSV	1

Six

MODULE INTERFACES

The individual modules of a program, when linked together communicate with each other by passing data or groups of data. This passing is achieved by giving to the lower level module the name of each of the areas which are to be known to the called module (note — in practice it is the addresses of the areas which are passed — for a detailed explanation of the workings of inter-module linkage *see* Chapter 12). Before a module can be specified it is necessary to be aware of the data areas that modules will need to be able to perform the processing required of them.

The next stage of modularisation is therefore to write down for each proposed module the names of the data areas that module will expect to have passed to it. This can be done as a straight list as shown below or the already drawn module linkage chart can be annotated. Writing the data names on the linkage chart makes some of the checks described below easier but can be confusing if the chart is small or if the number of modules/data names is large. The choice is largely a matter of preference.

Proposed module	Data areas required
Read/Validate card D20	card input area, indicator
Deletions routine	input transaction, input master, output deletions area
Exceptions routine	error record area, indicator, print-area

A number of useful checks can now be carried out using the module linkage chart and the list of required data areas, i.e. a list of the interfaces between the various modules.

The first point to check is that the overall framework of the program is logically correct. In other words we wish to ensure that the framework established by the modules on the linkage chart corresponds exactly to the framework established by the data areas on the same linkage chart. It is very easy, and not uncommon, to have these two

30

frameworks out-of-phase giving a final program structure that is cumbersome and inefficient because the original design was illogical. This type of mistake will normally only occur in very large programs with a great many modules; the example below to show this error represents only a small part of the large program.

Imagine a data area C split into two segments A and B. Segment B contains a sub-segment known as D (Figure 6.1). In this linkage chart

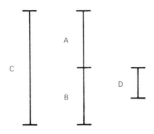

Figure 6.1

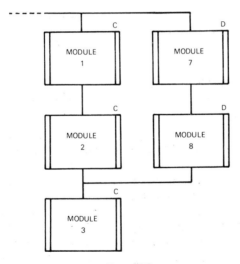

Figure 6.2

modules 1, 2 and 3 require area C whilst modules 7 and 8 require area D. However, because module 3 (called by module 8) requires area C it will be necessary to pass area C to modules 7 and 8 also (Figure 6.2).

31

This is of course permissible but the fact that it occurs should be taken as a signal to examine the structure of this area with a view to possibly redesigning it so that either module 8 does not link with 3 or if it does then the areas required are already available in the calling modules. The example quoted above also highlights the next check to be made on the module interface chart. It is essential that areas to be passed to a module are available in the calling module. Consider this sequence with the required parameters alongside each module (Figure 6.3). When module

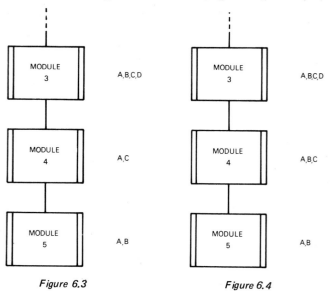

Figure 6.3   Figure 6.4

3 calls module 4 it has available the required parameters A and C and no problems occur. However, although module 4 does not use data area B it is required to pass this area to module 5. It will be necessary therefore for module 3 to pass data area B to module 4 so that it can be passed to module 5 (Figure 6.4). When the data areas are distinct groups then this type of omission in the definition of interfaces is easy to spot. However, when subsidiary modules require subsidiary areas it is possible to mistakenly think the area is missing and pass an extra parameter (Figure 6.5). Area D is not passed by name to module 2 although it is available there since it is a subsidiary area to data area C. Passing parameters of C and D to module 2 would work but would introduce redundant code and would almost certainly prove confusing to anyone reviewing the program some time after it was written.

32

Normally one would expect that the parameters passed down a linkage chart will follow a hierarchical structure similar to the logic of the modules. The lower down a module linkage chart one goes the

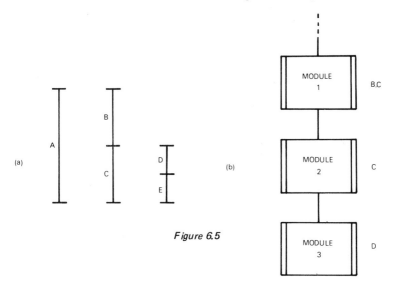

Figure 6.5

smaller the logic becomes relative to the overall program logic. In the same way the data areas passed to lower level modules will normally be smaller relative to the overall data areas assigned to the program. Figures 6.6 and 6.7 illustrate an ideal hierarchical structure of data areas. In this chart the small areas are already grouped into the large

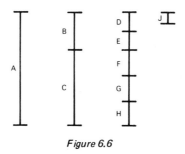

Figure 6.6

data area A. However, in some cases a linkage chart may be produced showing a large number of non-contiguous areas passed to each of several modules. A very long parameter list is undesirable for two reasons.

33

The major reason is the possibility of error in transcribing the list when coding the modules. It is very easy to write down a long list either out-of-order or with an entry missing; this type of error although quite simple can be extremely difficult to detect during the testing stages. The second reason for avoiding long strings of parameters is the limitation placed on the length of such lists by some high-level language compilers. Certain Cobol compilers, for example, generate a considerable

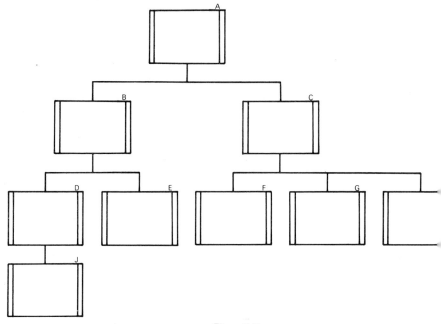

Figure 6.7

amount of extra coding if a parameter string is presented containing more than five entries.

When a linkage chart has long lists of parameters it is worthwhile therefore looking at the areas with a view to joining them together to form one large contiguous area. For example, a Print-Output module may be passed a number of parameters identifying the print-line, line and page counts and several heading lines. It would be a simple task to combine the several heading lines into a single area and to combine the print-line with the various counts; the number of parameters being reduced therefore to two.

34

LEVELS OF DEFINITION

Now that the areas required by each module are clearly defined and
verified it is possible to decide at which level in the hierarchy each
data area should be defined. A data area must be defined at or before
the highest level at which it appears. For example, if an area is passed
to a module at the fourth level it must be defined at the third level or
above (Figure 6.8). A data area to be passed to module 5 must be

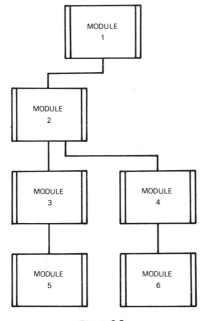

Figure 6.8

defined in module 3 or above. If the area to be passed to module 5
was also to be passed to module 6 then the area would have to be
defined in module 2 (level 2) or above.

It is clear that to avoid the problems of selecting the correct level of
definition and the possibility of wrong-level definition all the data areas
could be defined at the highest level. So far our knowledge of modular
programming would select this highest level as the control module. To
define all the data areas in the control module is a widely used and
advantageous technique; however, even this can be improved upon by
creating a higher level module to contain only data areas.

THE DATA MODULE

A data module is one which will contain all the data areas required for a program. This module will be called by Job Control or the Loader and will do no processing other than to call the control module and to stop

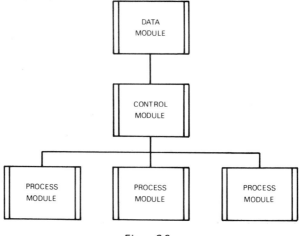

Figure 6.9

the run when control is returned to it. A program may contain only one data module which will always be at the highest level in the module linkage structure (Figure 6.9). The use of the data module has a number of advantages as well as some disadvantages. Both are discussed below.

Advantages of the Data Module Technique

The testing of modules within a program will always be easier with a data module in use. Since all the data areas will be external to all the modules under test it is a simple matter to test modules requiring files without actually having to set up a file (Figure 6.10). When this process module is being tested it is not necessary for the I/O module to be present and therefore not necessary to have the relevant file available. The area used by the I/O module for the current record to be stored is passed to the process module. The area can therefore be primed with a dummy record prior to entry of the process module. The same will hold true for the structure shown in Figure 6.11. The

36

control module of a program now becomes very like a process module and can be tested in the same way. The testing of modules (using test harnesses) is discussed in some detail in Chapter 10.

The maintenance of program structures becomes a lot easier when using a data module because it is only necessary to alter one module (the data module) when amending the structure of a data area. It is

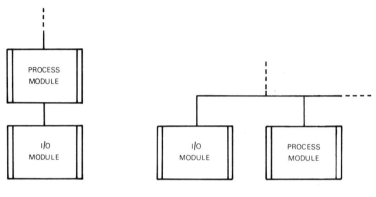

Figure 6.10   Figure 6.11

also easier to add a lower level module to a structure since the data areas it requires are automatically available in the module which is to call it. If a data module were not in use the addition of a lower level module to the program structure could entail the amendment of all the intermediate modules to make available the required data area(s) to the new module. A data module structure cannot normally be passed to a standard module since the data module layout varies from program to program and the standard module is generalised. However, it is quite permissible to pass only a sub-set of the data module to any process module requiring it. This should only be done to the lowest level or to a closed (i.e. last in line) module when the possibility of adding a lower level module is remote. Most standard modules will be of the closed type and can always therefore fit into a program using the data module technique without any trouble (Figure 6.12). In this case the entire data module area is passed to all the modules except the standard module. Only that data area required by the standard module is passed to it. Note that an evolved type of standard module should be specified in such a way that it receives only the data areas required by it and is closed.

Determining the best method, if any, of overlaying a modular program is discussed in detail in Chapter 8. However, it is clear that active data (data that maintains a value between executions of a module) cannot be overlayed. In a normal program structure this can present a number of difficulties if it is found that the completed program will not fit into the core space available. With a data module, however,

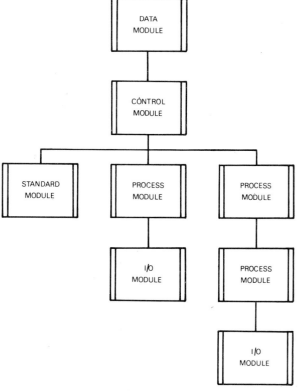

Figure 6.12

all the active data is automatically in one place and provided the data module resides in the Root Phase (*see* Glossary) any module or group of modules can be overlayed at any time during the execution of the program.

The problems associated with large parameter strings are discussed earlier in this chapter. Their use is avoided by the incorporation of a data module into the program structure. In addition to the potential error of transcribing parameter strings is the possibility of mistranscribing the layout of the data areas themselves. It only requires one field near the beginning of a data area to be given an incorrect length for the remainder of the area (perhaps containing a large number of individual fields) to be out of alignment.

This problem is easily overcome when the operating system contains a facility for cataloguing groups of source statements to a library for subsequent retrieval during compilation. An example of this is the use of the Cobol **COPY** verb. Each data area required in the data module is defined and carefully described in source language cards which are then catalogued to the Source Statement Library. Each module requiring the layout of any of these areas can then **COPY** it exactly into itself with the minimum of effort and the maximum of reliability. If a language does not contain the copy feature then a preprocessor can be written or bought (e.g. PLIP for PL/1) or the required cards can be physically duplicated each time they are required (although this latter technique is not recommended).

When a large program is to be developed and it is to have a data module it is a good idea to allocate this responsibility to one of the senior members of the team. At the commencement of development a skeleton data module has to be drawn up with all the main file areas and known accumulators, etc., together with a large area set aside for working—storage, hash totals, etc. As each member of the team requires a work area or store for his module he will request it from the Senior Programmer. In this way duplication of storage space is avoided and the data module definition is kept up-to-date.

Disadvantage of the Data Module Technique

Once a program is complete or is at an advanced stage of testing an amendment of the structure of a data area may mean the recompilation or assembly of all the other modules in the program (since they all use the same data area layout). Fortunately, this disadvantage can be overcome by making the field to be changed redundant and adding the revised field to the end of the data area. (The discussion later of work-ings of Modular Programming will make it clear how this is possible.) This method of avoiding recompilation cannot be applied to file record layouts but once these have been specified they should not require any changes.

The data module for the case study would contain five areas:

1 for each main file; 1 work area (record counts, print line, headings, constants, status indicators, etc.)

Each module (except standard modules) would therefore have five parameters passed to it.

Seven

PROGRAMMING LANGUAGES AND USE OF STAFF

The choice of programming language for a given program specification
is usually governed by an installation standard and does not enter the
realm of the modulariser. Most commercial installations using third
generation equipment will have chosen to use a high-level language
(Cobol, PL/1) because of the reduction in development costs that could
be expected from its use. However, there are occasions when either a
programming language is not specified in the installation standards or
the modulariser has reason to suppose that the specified language is not
suitable for a particular module or modules. Often when the installation
standards are to be deviated from it is necessary to obtain permission
from a departmental manager; when this is the case it is essential that
the arguments presented for the choice of language(s) are sufficient to
convince those who will make the final decision.

There are a number of reasons why a high-level language (or the
installation standard language) may be unsuitable for a particular
module. The most common reason is that the normal language is either
unable to handle the particular function required by the module or
although it will handle the function it does so in such an inefficient
manner as to be unacceptable. Some of the more common of these
functions are discussed below.

As discovered in Chapter 5, most file handling modules will be
standard ones and will not normally be scheduled for a run-of-the-mill
program. However, the design of a file handling module must be done
at some time. Some high-level languages cannot handle certain types of
file organisation such as Indexed Sequential or Direct Access, or if they
can handle them, do so in a very inefficient manner. It may be necessary
therefore to elect to program some or all of these modules in a
low-level or assembly language. This will be particularly true in the
case of a direct access file requiring complicated computations to
arrive at a physical device address from which a record is to be read.

Some installations, because of economic considerations, require to install peripherals manufactured by a different company to that which manufactured their Central Processor. In this case it is almost certain that the high-level language(s) provided by the computer manufacturer will not be capable of interfacing with this new device. Once again it will be necessary to revert to an assembly language to establish communication with the odd-ball peripheral. Similarly, most high-level languages do not, as yet, provide facilities for communicating with remote or teleprocessing devices. Even if a high-level language can handle a single teleprocessing device it will almost certainly not have facilities for producing the re-entrant coding normally required to handle a large number of remote devices. It is not uncommon to see Cobol programmers struggling to code a simple mathematical equation. Although Cobol has the basic arithmetic operators (add, subtract, divide, multiply), it is not designed for complex expressions. The performance of mathematical (as opposed to arithmetic) calculations is best done in a language designed for the job such as Fortran. As well as simplicity in the coding of mathematical expressions, Fortran has also the advantage of built-in functions for computing such things as sine, cosine and square root values. Although basically for scientific problems Fortran can have its uses in a commercial installation and it is well worth while having at least one programmer conversant with its principles.

PROBLEMS OF MIXED LANGUAGES

The above discussion presents valid reasons for mixing the programming languages used in a single program but it is important to bear in mind also the disadvantages of mixed languages. When faced with a requirement for a low-level or non-standard language in a high-level installation the points discussed below should be considered carefully before finally selecting a language for the module. The problems posed may well be so great as to indicate that the system should be redesigned to remove the low-level or non-standard requirement.

All languages available under a given operating system should use the same inter-module linkage system to ensure compatibility. This, however, is not always the case and certain languages (such as Cobol and PL/1) may not be able to communicate freely without having an intermediate assembler interface. This extra coding and development is clearly undesirable and should be avoided wherever possible.

It is very tempting for assembler programmers to use information from the supervisor or from file communication areas to try and improve their coding. This information is not officially available to the user and the manufacturer may at any system release decide to amend the format or layout of such areas. This could mean that every assembler module has to be checked for possible incompatibility every time the operating system is re-leased. Obviously, a complete waste of time. If low-level languages are to be used the programmers in the department must adhere to the installation standards and not use unofficial facilities.

A major problem with the use of low-level languages in an installation geared to a high-level choice is the continuance of a maintenance capability within the programming department. Turnover in programming staff is so great that an installation could suddenly find itself without any assembler expertise. In this case the potential disruption of development schedules is very easy to imagine. Closely allied to the maintenance dilemma is the enforcement of standards which have been designed for use with a high-level language and do not therefore cover all the eventualities arising with the use of low-level languages. This can be particularly irksome if the Senior Programmer or Team Leader responsible for a mixed language development is not himself conversant with all the languages being coded by his team.

The original specification of the Cobol language included the requirement that programs coded in the language should be completely independent of computer and operating system. Although this is not exactly the case it is certainly possible to amend a Cobol program to run on another machine or under another operating system with minimal changes. This also applies to languages such as Fortran and Algol and to PL/1 on IBM machines. It does not apply, however, to assembly languages which are peculiar to their own machine and even on the same hardware their macro language subsets can vary between operating systems. For an installation with long term plans to upgrade hardware and /or software these points should be borne in mind when developing program suites with potentially long lives.

Selection of Staff

This discussion is not related to the initial appointment of staff but to their assignment to various tasks within an overall project development plan. The distribution of modules within a programming department should be related as closely as possible to the different abilities of the staff available. The experience (and hopefully therefore the ability) of a programmer should relate to the difficulty of the task presented. A more experienced programmer should receive more difficult or more complex modules to develop. Providing this scheduling is done within the limits of availability it will maximise the utilisation of manpower and will improve the state of mind of programmers. It is a common mistake to schedule modules on an arbitrary basis, assuming them to be of equal difficulty, and so have some programmers bored with work that is too easy and others hot under the collar with difficult coding on a tight schedule.

The tremendous expansion of the computer industry at present with the consequent shortage of experienced staff emphasises the need to provide adequate and satisfying training. It is important therefore that the selection of modules for trainee staff to code is approached in a meaningful way. Many programmers had as their introduction to coding proper to code a specially devised test program. The trainee would be unlikely to put any enthusiasm into this job knowing that it was completely unproductive and had been coded by many before him. This training method is to be viewed as totally unacceptable in the present state of the industry; not only does it in no way motivate the beginner but, perhaps more important, it is completely unproductive. If installations are to build up loyalty amongst their programmers it is essential to give them job satisfaction and with rising overheads it is essential that all members of the programming department become productive at the earliest opportunity. Modular programming is a tremendous help in training since almost all programs will contain at least one simple module (such as one to build a print-line) which can readily be developed by a trainee straight back from his first course. In this way job satisfaction is provided since the trainee immediately feels useful and will learn something of the art of programming and the installation will recover the cost of his training quite soon.

Within a given level of difficulty of module several different functions may be apparent. These should be distributed as widely as possible in the relevant stratum of ability in order to broaden the coding experience of each programmer. However, in order to maintain the shortest possible development time it is important to identify and make use of relevant skill or experience possessed by one or more programmers. For example a particular programmer may have already coded several core sort

44

routines in which case he should be given any more which arise unless another programmer can do it without increasing the overall development time.

If the allocation of modules has been completed before their specifications have been produced then the specifications can be tailored to the recipient. A trainee programmer will require quite a detailed specification covering all the logical requirements together with a macro flow-chart of the processing to be performed by the module. A senior programmer on the other hand can usually work from an outline specification giving only the overall objective of the module.

Eight

USE OF CORE STORAGE

With the increasing use of high-level languages many programmers are finding difficulty containing their program size within the available core storage. Despite claims made by manufacturers, high-level languages do tend to use considerably more core than the equivalent written in a low-level language. Some Cobol compilers for example include a fixed overhead of 1K of core for every module written. Clearly in a large program with many modules this could be a severely limiting factor.

Most people are prepared to accept the increased core requirements of high-level language programs because they are offset to a considerable degree by decreased development costs. In addition to this the trend over the last few years has been for the cost of core storage to be continually and significantly reduced enabling installations to have much larger central processor configurations without too much extra cost. These two factors would seem to balance out leaving computer departments in a reasonably happy situation with large (slightly inefficient) high-level language programs being loaded into large areas of core storage. Unfortunately for the programmer, however, this is not the case. Parallel advances in other software areas have meant that the hardware size is no longer the only limiting factor in the size of one program. Most programmers will be quite used to having a Supervisor or Executive residing in low core claiming perhaps 15–20 per cent of the total available core storage space. However, in order to increase the throughput of modern central processors delayed so much by slow peripherals it has been necessary to develop multi-programming. This involves more than program residing in core at any one time with the Supervisor handing control to the highest priorty program that is not awaiting the completion of a peripheral operation. In order for this to be done it has been necessary to divide up the non-supervisor area of core into partitions. Each partition can therefore hold one program at any one time.

In the case of an installation only doing spooling in addition to the normal batch production work, the extra partitions required would be quite small. However, if some form of teleprocessing application was to be on-line then the batch program may find itself with a much reduced area to work in (*see* Figure 8.1). We now find that instead of

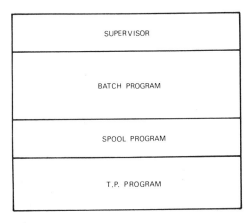

Figure 8.1

having 80—85 per cent of the total core storage the batch program may have less than 50 per cent. In this case it is clear that, despite large amounts of cheap core, some batch processing programs will be too large for the available partition. It is necessary then to introduce an overlay structure into the program in order that it can be run in the available partition. It would be disastrous to the installation to allow one program to use all available core because of the potential disruption to schedules caused by having to abandon a spooling run. A request to introduce overlays into a monolithic program would usually be greeted by hysteria at least. To attempt to overlay a program written without this in mind is one of the most difficult if not impossible tasks that can be presented to a programming department.

The introduction of overlays into a modular program is a completely different story. Without any planning at the modularisation stage it is an easy task but if a few simple rules are observed at this stage then overlaying becomes almost a matter of routine.

The important consideration when implementing overlays is to ensure that no active modules or active data are overlayed. Active in this sense can be defined as meaning still in use. A module is activated when

47

control is transferred to its entry point and it remains active until it returns control, via its return point, to its calling module. The hidden snag here is to realise that a module remains active when it passes

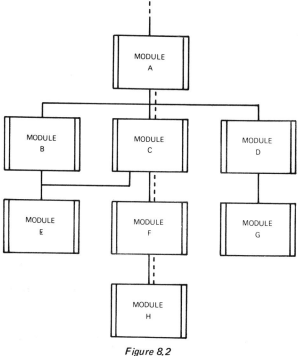

Figure 8.2

control to a lower level module. Consider Figure 8.2. (The dotted line through modules A, C, F and H represents the intial calling sequence.)

The control module A will remain active throughout the execution of the program. When module A calls module C, modules A and C are both active. Similarly when C calls F and F calls H this results in modules A,C,F and H all being active at the same time. Since a called module can be considered as a subroutine of the calling module it is easy to accept that the calling module remains active although it has passed control to a lower level.

When module H returns control to module F then module H is deactivated. Similarly module F returning control to module C will deactivate module F. If module C now calls module E then the currently active modules are A, C and E. Note that although E can be called by module B it is possible for module E to be active without module B being so.

A major cause of mistake in overlaying is to fail to appreciate that a deactivated module can contain active data. Suppose that module H above is used to format and output information to a line printer, its working storage areas will therefore contain such information as line and page counts and if this module was overlayed this information would be lost and every fresh overlay would reset the counts to one. This cannot be allowed to happen but obviously an overlay restriction on a module at the lowest level could introduce considerable undesirable complications into the overlay structure. The simple solution is to remove the working storage from all the modules and place it in a high level module that will not be overlayed. In other words use the data module concept (*see* Chapter 6).

When attempting to locate all active data in a data module it is important to examine all the modules containing I/O routines. Most of these modules will contain some form of file communication area (DTF, FD, DECLARE FILE, DCB) each of which will contain active data (flags, record counts, etc.) for as long as the file to which they refer is active (i.e. for as long as the file is Open).

OVERLAYING

In order that sections of a program can be overlayed it is necessary to divide that program into phases. A phase is defined as a relocatable module or group of relocatable modules composed or linked together to form a loadable routine.

A phase may be loaded into a fixed (i.e. pre-determined) area of core or it may be dynamically relocatable and loadable into different areas of core under control of the resident part of the program. Whether the dynamic relocatability feature is available will depend upon the software in use. A phase will reside in a System Library, which will normally be a Direct Access Storage Device, from where it can be brought into core on request by the System Loader. A phase can be of two types, a Root phase or an Overlay phase.

A root phase is defined as one that is loaded into core at the beginning of a program and remains there until the program is terminated. A program may contain only one root phase which will communicate with the operating system.

A program may of course contain more than one permanently resident phase but only that one communicating with the operating system will be called a root phase.

An overlay phase is one that is loaded into core during execution of the program to overwrite another overlay phase and/or is overwritten by another overlay phase. A program may contain several hundred overlay phases each of which is loaded once only and is overwritten by the next one or it may contain only two overlay phases which constantly overlay each other depending upon the required information processing.

Figure 8.3 illustrates the structure of an overlay program. The root phase, as already explained, resides in core throughout the execution of the program and is not therefore overlayed. Phases 1 and 2 overlay each

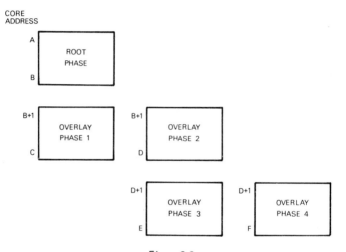

Figure 8.3

other and cannot therefore have concurrently active modules. Similarly modules in phases 3 and 4 cannot be active at the same time. However, a module in phase 3 can be active with either phase 1 or phase 2 depending upon the module linkage structure in use.

Although overlaying a program may enable it to run without extensive reprogramming it can introduce severe time penalities. The extra efficiency obtained by enabling multi-programming to be introduced may be completely offset by the degradation of running time in a badly overlayed program. To introduce an overlay phase from the systems library can take upwards of 300 ms and with a bad design resulting in say several overlays for each record on a file this can mount

50

up rapidly. The following overlay design points should therefore always be borne in mind. The root phase must contain all permanently active modules and data, this will include the data module (if used), the control module, any modules with permanently active data (i.e. I/O modules).

Ideally the routines to be overlayed should be those which are used infrequently or once only such as initialisation, end of run and abort procedures. Unfortunately it is not always possible to limit the overlays to those routines and it is necessary therefore to produce overlay phases which will be changed as seldom as possible. This can usually be done by tracing on the module linkage chart the likely calling sequences of the modules. Clear patterns will normally be apparent of groups of modules which are always used together. Each of these groups can become an overlay phase. An example of this would be in a file update program where different overlay phases could be produced to deal with additions, deletions and amendments. If the transaction file for this program could be pre-sorted using the transaction type as one of the keys, then the amount of overlaying required would be considerably reduced.

This type of approach could be applied to the Case Study if an overlay arrangement was required. The root phase would contain the data and control modules together with the I/O modules including the print module (even though this is at the lowest level of other overlay phases it can be in the root phase). Other phases could then be made up of each of the add, delete, update, month end and exception routines or combinations of these depending upon core requirements and usage.

PROGRAM VARIATION

Overlay procedures can be used to provide variations of standard programs for use on special occasions. An update program can be converted to a file set-up program by overlaying the amendment phase. A more useful application is a selective print program designed to select records from a file satisfying certain parameters and then produce some form of print-out. By overlaying the printing phase of this program completely different reports can be produced at will. Considerable effort is saved here by utilising the file access and parameter match routines as a standard routine without having the system library cluttered with several programs.

Nine

TESTING REQUIREMENTS AND SPECIFICATIONS

This chapter is concerned not with the methods of testing modules but with the influence future testing can have on the design of the module linkage chart and on the schedule of module development.

The area most likely to cause set-backs in the testing is that concerned with input/output module development. It is this area then which should be examined first in order that the necessary schedules can be correctly drawn up. The splitting off of I/O into separate modules has already been examined; however, for anyone still not convinced the following should be sufficient.

Suppose a program reads a complex Direct Access file and the processing to handle this file is included in a module performing a number of functions. In order that this module can be tested it is necessary that the file is available; however, it is quite possible that some difficulties are being encountered in establishing it (for example, the routine to write the file may not yet be ready). Even if the file can be created it will be a time consuming exercise to produce data for each routine to be tested. If, however, the file handling routine had been designed as a separate module the testing of our original processing module becomes a significant amount easier. There are two methods by which the lack of direct access file can be made good. If the actual processing paths of the module can be tested without the use of a file, then a dummy module can replace the file handler. (A dummy module is one having only an entry point and a return point.) Alternatively, if the processing module requires different records from the direct access file each time it is executed then a substitution module can be used. In this case the substitution module could be coded to read cards and present them to the calling module as if a record had been read from the direct access file.

The substitution module technique can ease other testing problems also. A module or group of modules designed to output print images to a tape may be slightly troublesome if testing failures cause the tape to be left unclosed. Additionally, extra computer testing time is required to rewind the tape and print out the results for each test. However, if a direct print substitution module is used none of these problems will occur.

Problems encountered during testing can often be easily avoided by careful consideration at the modularisation stage. As a simple example take the case of a module designed to process a certain class of record that is grouped together on a file. The module is entered when the first record of the class is encountered and will exit when the first non-class record is read. The flow diagram for the module could look similar to that shown in Figure 9.1. Two problems can occur when testing this

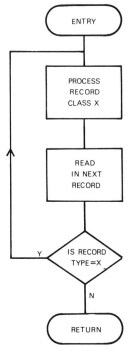

Figure 9.1

module. Firstly the module to read the input file might not be available, which introduces the problems mentioned earlier. Secondly to test the module with different sequences of input file (essential to ensure a 100 per cent test) would require several different input test files to be created. This could involve the programmer in a considerable amount of effort and could itself become a stumbling block to progress requiring its own development schedule!

If the module linkage chart is redesigned such that the reading of the file is no longer done in this module but perhaps in the control

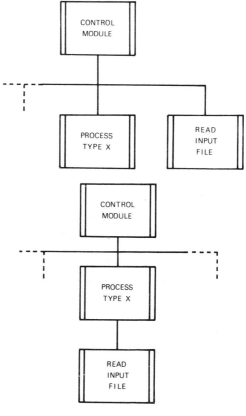

Figure 9.2

module the testing becomes considerably easier (Figure 9.2). The process module is now no longer dependent upon the sequence of the input file since it only deals with a single record at a time rather than a class of records. It will not be necessary therefore when testing this process module to supply more than one sequence on the input file. Furthermore since the record area is external to the process module (and can therefore be primed with any desired data) it is not even necessary to have an

54

input file to test the module! The exact method of testing this module now will be seen in Chapter 10.

When checking-out any test shots one must examine the result fields to ascertain if the module has functioned correctly and it is often necessary to be aware of the input to the module. To make this function simpler module linkages should be designed to include separate input and output areas for each module. This will facilitate easy verification of results and will enable any error in the input data to be readily identified. In addition separate areas mean that when a module is being repeatedly tested it is only necessary to reformat those areas which are required to be different from the preceding test. If a calculation routine module produces results in floating point data it is worthwhile specifying the output in packed or zoned decimal. The extra processing time required to change the scale of a number is negligible compared with the potential saving in check-out time. As a general rule the input and output areas of a module should be designed to enable easy checking.

The final testing consideration is required when the program development schedule is drawn up. Wherever possible modules on the lowest level should be completed first. This will ease the testing of modules on higher levels since it will not be necessary to supply dummy lower level modules. If a comprehensive test harness is in use this require-ment may no longer apply (*see* Chapter 10).

MODULE SPECIFICATION

The modulariser has at this point produced his final Module Linkage Chart and has decided the function of each module, who will write it and in what language. The next task is to produce specifications for each module which can be passed to the programmers for coding. We have already seen how the contents of a module specification will vary depending upon the level of experience of the recipient; however, they will also vary on the type of module. For example, it will not be neces-sary to include a flowchart when specifying a module to output a print-image to a line printer. The complexity or completeness of each specification will be unique to the module, but there are a number of requirements for a complete specification from which the modulariser can select those he requires. These requirements are discussed below.

Module Name

This is the name by which the module will be known to the programmers and the name which will be used in any department index of
modules (*see* Chapter 5). This name will not be known to the operating
system and should not therefore be a mnemonic. Examples of module
names are 'SORT PAYCHECKS INTERNALLY', 'VERIFY CHECK
DIGIT', etc.

Module Identity

This is the name by which the module will be known to the operating
system, i.e. the name by which it will be CALLed. The length and
format of this name will usually be restricted by the operating system
in use. For example on some 360s a module name must begin with
an alphabetic character and it must be no more than eight characters
in length.

A module identity can be made up in a number of ways depending
upon the departmental preference or standards. A common method is
to use (hopefully) meaningful mnemonics to identify the function, e.g.
'CHKDIG', 'PRNTLIN', 'CLRTOTS'. Unfortunately, producing different
but recognisable mnemonics becomes quite difficult as the number of
modules in use increases and an instantly identifiable name to one
programmer may be completely meaningless to another. A more
organised system is to build up module identities on a pre-set pattern,
the result of which will identify the module's origin and currency at a
glance. For example, the identity could be built up as follows:

Digits 1—4 —program to which module belongs
Digit 5   —author code
Digits 6—7 —module number within program
Digit 8   —version number of module

For example, 'AR37C202' would identify the second version of module
20 in program AR37 coded by programmer C. A similar system could
be used for identifying standard modules.

Module Function

This is a brief outline of the function of the module, e.g.'roll up
monthly totals and zeroise this months'. This requirement is often
satisfied by the module name and can therefore be frequently omitted.

Source Language

The language in which the module is to be coded. This need only be specified if different from the installation standard.

Linkage Details

This is a list of the parameters to be passed to this module, in their correct order, showing their size (i.e. length) and format. Any external areas, not passed in a parameter string, but used by this module should also be identified.

Parameters

MASTER RECORD AREA	120	A
CUSTOMER CODE	8	P
CURRENT TRANSACTION	28	A

(*Note.* Format codes indicate A — alphameric, P — packed decimal.)

Calling Examples

This can be omitted if the linkage details are considered adequate but otherwise is an example of a Call Statement to this module.

    CALL 'THISMOD' (MSTRREC, CUSCODE, TRANS);   (PL/1)

Flowchart

The complexity and number of flowcharts required, if any, is directly related to the complexity of the module and the ability of the recipient (if known). Usually only a general macro flowchart is required. If a very detailed micro flowchart is found to be necessary then consideration should be given to splitting down of this module into more, smaller, modules.

57

Processing Notes

This is a brief, but unambiguous, explanation of the processing to be done by this module with reference, where necessary, to the flowchart. For a simple module with a good flowchart this section may be omitted.

Called Modules

This is a list of other modules available to this module to perform some of the functions required of it. This list may seem superfluous when a module library exists but it is a useful documentation reference when setting up testing arrangements.

Module Diagram

This is a small 'black box' drawing showing the file(s) and external core areas, if any, **referenced by this module**. If the module is purely a process type this section may be omitted. Note, however, that a module reading a file via another module is logically referring to that file itself.

The following sample module specification should illustrate clearly the points discussed above.

Module Name — Read and Validate Card.

Module Identity — S213DTCD.

Module Function — To read a single card and check that it conforms to the requirements laid down in App. 3 of the Systems Guide.

Source Language — Assembler.

Linkage Details — Parameters Card Area   80 A
                                    Indicator   1 X

Calling Example — CALL 'S213DTCD' USING CARD—AREA,
                                    STATUS—BYTE—1 (COBOL).

58

Flowchart

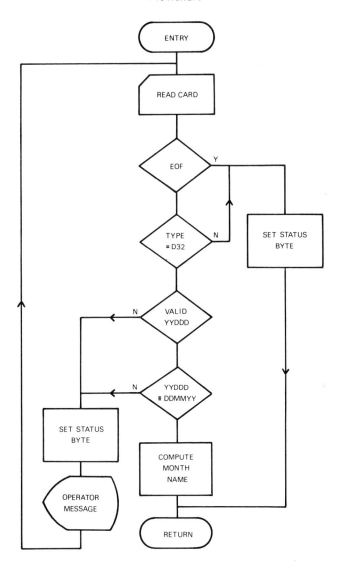

Figure 9.3

Processing Notes — Read a single card, if no card or not type D32 set status byte bit 2 and 3 ON, exit. If type D32 check columns 4—14 for validity as described in App. 3 of Systems Guide, if invalid set status byte bit 5. ON inform operator of invalidity and await new card. If dates valid look up month name and insert in columns 20—32 of card image.

Called Modules — 'SO4MNTH' USING month-no, month-name this module inserts name of month if month no is in range 1—12.

Module Diagram

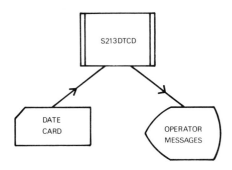

Figure 9.4

60

Ten

TESTING TECHNIQUES

After each module has been coded it is necessary to test it individually
before linking with other modules to form the complete program.
However, the very nature of a module introduces difficulties in testing
since it cannot, on its own, be loaded into the computer and neither
can it be executed. In order for the module to be loaded into a computer
it must first be link-edited or composed into a phase. However, even
when this is done the module cannot always be tested since most will
be written expecting to be called by a higher level module. Therefore not
only must the module be linked into a phase but it must also be provided
with some form of temporary driver routine to simulate its calling.
There are a number of ways these two requirements can be obtained
and each is explained below.

Standard Test Harness

A number of Software Houses offer software packages designed as a
module testing aid available for a number of operating systems. These
routines are by their nature generalised, but the concepts involved in
modular programming usually mean that this is not a limiting factor in
the usability of such packages. When considering the purchase of a
module test package, the user should consider not only the testing
requirements discussed below, but also the limitations, if any, posed
by the package in the use of alternative languages and/or operating
systems.

Installation Standard Test Harness

It is of course quite feasible for an installation to design and write its
own module tester with all, if not more, of the facilities available from

packages. There are, however, inherent dangers in this particular approach. An installation new to modular programming will not be able to call upon the wealth of experience of the subject available to the Software House and will probably not have the expertise available to write an efficient testing program. A self-written test harness will almost certainly cost more than a purchased package to produce and if it is inefficient it will cost more to run. Despite the foregoing remarks it is often a good idea for an installation to write its own module tester. This particularly applies in a very large department with unusual testing requirements.

Project Standard Test Harness

This is effectively a sub-set of the installation test harness discussed above since it will normally involve fewer options and facilities. Although development costs will therefore be reduced for this type of tester, they will of course be repeated for each project.

Temporary Alteration

A large proportion of modules written can be amended for the purpose of testing by, for example, the addition of I/O routines. Although this method is cheap and relatively quick it is not recommended since it introduces the further possibility of error when the module is restored to its original condition.

Combination into Phases

When all the modules of a program are coded they can be combined into a program and this can be tested in the normal manner. To do this as the normal method of module testing would of course defeat the whole object of modular programming, although the technique will be used in the final stages of program testing.

The choice of testing method should be made bearing in mind a number of important factors which, if ignored, could offset the advantages gained from Modular Programming. These factors, which are self-explanatory, are listed below:

   (1) Ease of use

   (2) Flexibility

(3) Ease of production of comprehensive test data
(4) Ease of result checking
(5) Ease of amendment of test data
(6) Potential error rate
(7) Ease of control
(8) Level of expertise of users
(9) Compatibility with installation standards
(10) Reduction in machine-time usage
(11) Programmer effort required

It is clear from the foregoing that the ideal method of testing lies in the purchase of a proprietary software package. Once such a package has been selected the programmer is relieved of a large portion of the repetitive, and therefore error-prone, work involved in testing modules. Since all the programmer now has to do is provide test data and a few simple control cards, he is able to devote more time to the important task of ensuring that his module is thoroughly tested.

MODULE TESTING IN PRACTICE

Before looking at the practical testing requirements it is worthwhile to reiterate the basic qualities of modules. A module will (1) perform one basic function, (2) be easily comprehended in total, (3) be small, (4) have few process paths, (5) process a small amount of data.

Providing the module under test satisfies all the points above it will be possible, and indeed desirable, to test every process path within the module over the full range of maximum and minimum values. If all the modules in a program are 100 per cent tested and working then it is a relatively simple task to combine them correctly and produce a program test that is 100 per cent correct.

The first stage in the production of module test data is therefore to examine the module flowchart to determine the total number of possible process paths through the module. Consider the flowchart shown in Figure 10.1 for a module to calculate the number of days in the year to a given date. At first glance this module would appear to have six process paths, but if the first tested condition is true then so will the second be true (if month = 1 it is also less than 3). The module has therefore only four process paths. In order to test every path the following dates could be submitted to the module:

01	01	57
31	12	69
11	02	72
21	03	72

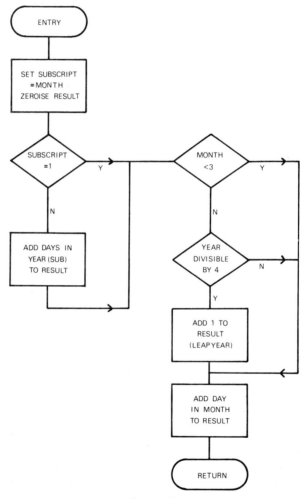

Figure 10.1

In addition to testing all the process paths these values cover the maximum and minimum value of days within the year. If the calling module does not validate the date prior to passing it to this module, then it would also be necessary to supply erroneous data to confirm that the module had working error condition coding.

When testing a module that performs calculations it is very important that the intermediate result fields are examined to ensure that sufficient space has been allowed. Once this has been done test data must be so designed as to test not only the maximum and minimum values but also combinations of these. Consider this calculation

$$\frac{A+B}{C} \times D = E$$

Each input value may only require one digit although the result could be three digits long:

$$\frac{9+9}{1} \times 9 = 162$$

In this case the intermediate result (prior to multiplication) was 18, which fits the result field. However, in the case

$$\frac{1+1}{9} \times 9 = 2$$

the result only requires one digit but the intermediate result is 0·22, requiring two decimal places.

The internal storage area of the module used for any intermediate results in this case will therefore need to be five positions in length with the right-hand two representing decimal places. Calculation modules must also be primed with a zero divisor if this is possible in a real operating environment to ensure that an abort condition is not raised. This condition is often overlooked when the divisor is itself the result of a calculation.

The basic rule to follow is to test a module with a full range of valid and invalid data and to ensure that the invalid input data does not produce an invalid output (usually in this case a flag bit can be set on).

MODULE SIMULATION

When testing at other than the lowest level the module under test may require to call a lower level module. However, it may be that this lower level module is not available for the purposes of testing, or is available but cannot practically be used.

Simulation of modules falls into two categories — the inclusion of a dummy module and the inclusion of a substitution module. A dummy module is one that performs no processing but merely returns control to the calling module immediately it is called. A dummy module serves therefore only to provide an entry point name without which the test run would be abandoned at link-edit or compose time. A dummy Cobol module is illustrated.

```
ENTER LINKAGE.
ENTRY 'DUMMY'.
ENTER COBOL.
ENTER LINKAGE.
RETURN.
ENTER COBOL.
```

A substitution module is one specially written to provide simple processing in place of a more complex variety in the original module. A good example of this is in the testing of a module which requires access, via a called module, to a complex direct access file. Because of the nature of this file, it may require a considerable amount of time and thought to set up a test version of it to enable the calling module to be tested. This is a waste of time and effort since the calling module (the one under test) only requires a (known) record to be passed to it, i.e. it does not need to test the file access module. A substitution module can therefore be coded to read cards and present these to the module under test as if it were a record from the direct access file.

Another use of the substitution module is when testing a module that calls a print module to output print lines to a tape for later spooling. During testing it is wasteful to output to tape and then print off the result; a substitution module written to output print lines direct to the lineprinter can be used instead.

Eleven

FURTHER TESTING

Once each individual module has been checked-out as described in the previous chapter it is necessary to produce a working program. Since all the modules are known to work the production of a working program requires only that the modules be linked together correctly and that they are called in the correct sequence. In other words the final stage of testing prior to producing a completed program is reduced to the task of checking-out the operation of the control module. The control module is tested in a different manner to the other modules since it does not normally have an entry point (in the case of a data module the two can be tested as one). However, since the control module will not be doing any processing we do not require to view the module's output. The main function of the control module is to direct the calling sequence of the other modules of the program.

The first test of a control module will therefore consist of a run with dummy modules with some means of identifying the fact that they have been called. Some of the proprietary packages available for module testing include special control module testing features. The control module is given an entry point (if it does not already have one) and all the lower level modules are dummied out. The package will trace the process flow through the control module by printing a diagnostic identifying each called module. If this trace feature is not available in the module tester in use then substitution modules can be used with a single print command (e.g. Cobol DISPLAY) to identify themselves. From this printout the logic path of the control module can be checked for validity remembering that the path traced out through the lower level modules should correspond to a macro flow-chart of the completed program.

The second stage of control module testing is to validate all the inter-module linkages and to ensure that all the data areas are correctly aligned across modules. Note that although these points have been checked at the modularisation stage they are a common area of error

67

and must be fully checked-out in a live condition before the program can be said to be complete.

The complete program is therefore linked (or composed) together and run with test data that is simple but designed to ensure that each module is called at least once by each of its calling modules. At this stage of testing logic errors within modules should not occur; if they do then the individual module testing procedures should be carefully examined for a lack of thoroughness.

Having now determined that each module functions as required and that linked together all the modules produce a program that works as required, it is necessary to ensure that the program specification has been interpreted as the Systems Analyst desired and that the program interfaces with other programs in the suite.

SUITE AND SYSTEMS TESTING

These two functions are often combined into a joint effort by the systems and programming departments although in a large organisation it may be preferable for the programming department to conduct independent suite testing before passing the programs over to the systems department. Suite testing is like program testing on a larger scale with each program regarded as a module and the object of the exercise being to ensure that all programs correctly interface with each other. Obviously the programs do not directly call each other but they do communicate via files of various kinds. Suite testing should therefore be designed to pass files containing all record types through the suite of programs to ensure that no incompatibilities occur within the various record layouts.

Systems testing should be designed to check not only the points outlined in suite testing above but also that the results of the programs are as predicted by the original specifications. Systems testing is designed therefore to supply all types of data to each program to ensure that not only is the data carried through from program to program successfully, but that it is processed as desired. As with any testing, systems testing must include a comprehensive range of invalid data.

Parallel running is not normally the province of the programming department since no program errors should occur at this stage. In fact if the foregoing testing suggestions have been adhered to the

68

parallel run of computer system to old method should produce
identical results leaving the suite available for production implementation
when desired.

PROGRAM MAINTENANCE

No matter how carefully the system has been designed or how well the
programs checked-out, production programs invariably require amendment from time to time. Reasons for program maintenance fall into two
broad categories. Either there has been discovered a fault in the original
coding of the program or a change in the specification has been requested
(either by the user department or by the systems department). There are
quite distinct areas and the method of program amendment should be
approached in distinct ways.

A program error will arise when there is a difference between the
function of the program and the intention of the program specification.
A program error can occur because the program was inadequately
tested or because the specification was wrong or ambiguous. In the
latter case the fault lies with the analyst who specified the program
originally; a programmer can be expected to identify logic errors in a
specification but he cannot be expected to recognise system inaccuracies.

The former case, caused by inadequate testing, is a very serious error
within the programming department and a thorough investigation must
be made in the hope that the mistake will not be repeated. The most
important area for investigation is the test data used to test that part
or module of the program that is suspect. Any program error that
manages to find its way through to a production program has usually
done so because the initial testing was inadequate and could not have
tested all the combinations of possibilities within the program. The
most common error is to assume that a program or module will not
receive rubbish data from an external source. Unless the specification
states that only valid data will be passed to a module then some form
of checking must be carried out otherwise the time is sure to come in
the production version when invalid data is given to the module only
to produce a program abort condition.

Once the results of the investigation into the program error are
known they should be widely circulated within the programming
department to ensure that a similar error does not lie hidden in another
production program.

A system change request will normally be made independently of the programming department and does not signify any failure on their behalf. Because of this it is not necessary to examine the causes of the request but merely to schedule the work into the departmental load depending upon the priority that can be attached to it. In order to reduce programming department overheads it is a good idea to stock-pile non-urgent system change requests until an 'economic batch quantity' is available when the programmer's time can be used to its best advantage.

Retesting

When a production program has to be amended it is essential to thoroughly retest all changed parts of the program prior to implementation. The particular module(s) that has been amended must be completely tested, with new test data if required, as if it was brand new. Having been satisfied that the changed module(s) is correct the programmer must link the new module into the program and re-do his link and suite testing. (Test data packs for this type of job can form part of the overall program documentation.) When this is complete the program can be parallel run with its original version and only when this is complete can the amended program be considered for production running.

Twelve

LINKAGE SYSTEMS

Most third generation machines have operand addresses in their machine instructions which consist of two parts — the base and the displacement. The base part identifies a general register which will contain, at execution time, a base or starting address. The base address can refer either to a program area or to a data area. The displacement is a count of the number of bytes between the base and the field being addressed. The absolute address of an operand is computed at execution time by adding the contents of the register to the displacement.

The base/displacement addressing mode enables the use of the concept of program relocatability. Since the base register is not initialised (i.e. set to the base address) until the program is loaded into core the program can be run in any part of core, without recompilation, providing the base register can be loaded dynamically. In other words, providing the start of the program can determine where in core it is without any outside assistance. This is normally achieved with a BALR R, O instruction which, it will be noted, does not itself require an initialised base register to function. The displacement portion of an address will remain constant during any execution and therefore any operands utilising a common base register will remain in the same relative positions to each other. It is quite common to see assembly language programs coded using a single base register for the program and the data areas. It is permissible (and indeed desirable) to use separate base registers for data areas.

A data area which has its own base register can be relocated during a single program run. The displacements for each of the fields within the data area remain constant since the layout of the area is fixed. If then the content of the data area base register is changed the relevant coding will be looking at another area in core with the same field layout. The only coding required to enable the program (or module) to 'look at' different areas of core is that establishing the base register. A module may assign several different base registers to cover a number of data areas and if the module is coded to initialise these base registers each time it is entered it becomes independent of any particular data areas.

Any program will require access to data either internal to the program or on an external storage device in order to complete its processing. Once the program is split into modules the data will need to be accessible by some or all of the modules. In order for a module to process a given area of data the data must reside in core and the module must be aware of the address of the data. If the data address is not known to the module at compile or assemble time (i.e. if the data is external to the module), then the data address must be communicated to the module at execution time.

There are four methods of communicating addresses across module boundaries although not all methods are supported by every programming language available. The choice of method will usually be determined by the Installation Standards, but if not the programmer, when making his choice, must remember that the efficiency of communication varies not only from method to method but also from language to language within the same method. The four methods are discussed below.

(1)   Parameter Strings

This is the most popular method of communication between modules and is supported by all languages and levels of operating system. This method involves passing to a lower level module a list of addresses each of which points to one data or parameter area. To communicate the list the address of the list itself is stored in a register prior to the call. Passing the address of the list rather than the individual addresses limits the use of registers and enables a list of any length to be passed. Conventionally register 1 is used to pass the address of the list. If the address list is to be variable in length the last entry can be signalled by setting on the lefthand (senior) bit in the lefthand byte.
Examples of method 1:

    CALL SUBMOD (A, B, C);   Fortran/PL/1

    CALL SUBMOD USING A, B, C   Cobol

72

```
        L 15, = V (SUBMOD)              BAL/Usercode
        LA    1, PARAMS
        BALR  14, 15



            .
            .
            .
            .

PARAMS DS     0F
       DC     A(A)
       DC     A(B)
       DC     A(C)
```

The advantages of this method are that it is very simple to use and it
allows data area space to be allocated once only (i.e. in the control
or data module).

The disadvantages of this method are mainly apparent in high-level
languages. Each time a call statement is used a block of coding will be
generated to establish the required address list even though it may have
been used previously. The number of parameters that can be passed is
limited by some high-level languages whilst others (e.g. PL/1) generate
descriptive tables of parameters which can waste valuable core storage.
This method of communication should only be used when the module
linkage chart depth-level does not exceed 3. If it is higher than this a
considerable amount of core storage can be wasted by the duplication
of address lists within different modules.

(2)   External Areas

This method is not supported by current Cobol compilers. An external
area is a contiguous area of core storage whose name is known to (i.e.
capable of being processed by) the linkage editor or composer. Since
the name is known at the link-edit or compose stage the run-time
address of the area can be relocated throughout all the modules
referencing the name. A module wishing to reference an external area
need only use the name in an external reference for the compiler or
assembler to indicate that this module requires an external name
resolution at link-edit or compose time. (Note that the external area

name is not passed from module to module.) An external area is identified by one of a number of keywords.

COMMON	Fortran
EXTERNAL	PL/1
ENTRY	BAL/Usercode
EXTRN	

An external area can be part of a module or it can be a module in its own right (i.e. data module).

This method of communication is also easy to use although some thought may be required about operating restrictions imposed by different linkage editors or composers. It is undoubtedly the most efficient means of communicating between modules since the address of each external area is held only once in each module and no actual coding is required to transfer the address at run-time. This method should be used wherever it is supported by the languages in use.

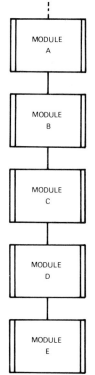

Figure 12.1

A major advantage of this method is the ease with which additional data areas may be communicated between modules. Consider the module structure shown in Figure 12.1. Suppose that a program specification amendment requires an additional area from module A to be communicated to module E. Using method 1 each of the modules in the structure (A, B, C, D and E) would require amendment to pass the new area down, but if external areas are in use then only modules A and E require amendment.

(3) Pointers

This method, which is supported by BAL/Usercode and PL/1, is a subset of method 2, and involves the creation of external lists of addresses which can be picked up and used to reference known data structures. This method has the advantage that there is no limit to the number of addresses in the list, and in PL/1 no dope-vectors are created. However, it requires more machine instructions per address than method 2.

(4) Registers

This method is supported only by BAL/Usercode and requires the absolute address of an area or an absolute value to be loaded into a general register immediately prior to the call statement. The called module can retrieve the value directly from the register, or, in the case of an address, can use the register as the base of the area to be processed. It is very fast but is not very flexible, is limited in the number of addresses that can be handled and may mean digression from the installation standards.

REMOTE AREA ADDRESSABILITY

We have seen how the addresses of parameters can be communicated to lower level modules but it is still necessary to establish addressability for these areas within the called module. In other words, it is necessary to pick-up the string of addresses, load them into registers and indicate to the compiler or assembler that these are the base addresses for these areas.

```
ENTRY 'SUBMOD' USING A, B, C                    Cobol

LM     4,6,0(1)                      BAL/Usercode
USING A,4
USING B,5
USING C,6


SUBMOD: PROCEDURE (A,B,C);                      PL/1
```

In Cobol and PL/1 the single statement used not only identifies the
number and position of the parameters but also the identity of the
module. This would be done in BAL/Usercode with a CSECT statement.
The detailed use of external areas is covered in Chapter 13.

MODULE BASE ADDRESS

In order that a module can be entered at run time the calling module
must know the entry point address to enable a branch to be made.
However, at the time the calling module is assembled or compiled the
address(es) of its called module(s) will not be available. The address(es)
will only become known when the complete program is link edited or
composed. When the assembler or compiler encounters an external
reference (i.e. a name that is not known to it) it will generate a V-type
address constant. On the assembly or compilation listing the content
of a V-type address constant is binary zero, but the object deck output
with the listing will contain a list of all unresolved external references.
One of the functions of the linkage editor or composer is to examine
these lists for each module and attempt to resolve each entry. Thus
if the name of the called module is known (i.e. if the called
module object deck has been included in the run) its run-time address
can be inserted in all the V-type address constants referring to it.
This V-type address constant can be loaded into a register (conventionally register 15) at run time and a branch made to it:

```
L     15, = V(SUBMOD)
BR    15
```

The called module will require an internal base register for its processing
instructions as well as for its remote data areas. Since register 15 will

76

contain the entry point address it can be used as the modules processing
base register:

```
SUBMOD CSECT
        USING    *, 15
```

Care must be exercised when using this technique since if the called
module becomes a calling module the contents of its base register (15)
will be destroyed when the call is made. It is necessary therefore in this
case to use an alternative register which can be initialised with the
contents of register 15:

```
SUBMOD CSECT
        USING    *, 3
        STM      14,12,12(13)
        LR       3,15
```

The USING statement (to indicate to the assembler which register will
be used as a base) must immediately follow the CSECT statement since
the address to be used is that of the CSECT. The LR to initialise the base
register must, however, follow the STM in order that the register used
will be correctly reset on return to the calling module (for a description
of register saving *see* Chapter 13). An alternative method of establishing
module addressability is:

```
SUBMOD  CSECT
        STM     14,12,12,(13)
        BALR    3,0
        USING   *,3
```

RETURN ADDRESS

For the called module to return control to the calling module at the
point from which the call came it must have a return address supplied.
This is conventionally supplied in register 14:

```
        L       15, = V (SUBMOD)
        LA      14,*+4+2+3*4
        BALR    1,15
        DC      A(A,B,C)
or      L       15, = V(SUBMOD)
        LA      1, ADDLST
```

```
BALR    14,15
```

```
ADDLST DC              A (A,B,C)
```

The called module can therefore return control to the calling module by initiating one simple branch:

```
BR      14
```

The high-level language equivalents will both basically generate a BR 14 also:

```
RETURN.                        Cobol
RETURN;                        PL/1
```

Thirteen

DATA AREAS

We have already seen how the address of a remote data area is passed to a called module but it is only an address; no attempt has been made to give the called module a description of the area in use. The area cannot be described at the same time as any internal areas since this would cause core storage to be reserved within the module and the references would then be to the internal rather than the external areas. Instead it is necessary only to give a layout of the area to the module such that it can be effectively used as a mask to lay over any part of core (by amending the base register). If the assembler or compiler has this mask and knows which register is to be used as a base for the area, then it can produce base/displacement values for references to any fields within the area. (Note the selection of base registers for remote areas in high-level language modules is done automatically.) Remote area masks are described differently in different languages.

Cobol

Remote parameter areas are described in the linkage section of a Cobol module. The method of description is identical with that used in the working storage section except that the VALUE clause is prohibited and no core storage is reserved. Each level 77 or level 01 entry in the linkage section must have a corresponding entry in the ENTRY statement at the logical beginning of the module. The level names do not have to be in the same sequence as the ENTRY parameters but there must be the same number with identical names. The calling module is expected to pass the parameter string in the same sequence as they appear in the ENTRY statement.

79

LINKAGE SECTION.

```
77              PARAMETER—B         PICTURE X(9).
01              PARAMETER—A.
                02 CODE             PICTURE 999.
                02 NAME             PICTURE X(20).
                02 ADDRESS          PICTURE X(30).
```

PROCEDURE DIVISION.

```
                ENTER LINKAGE.
                ENTRY 'SUBMOD' USING PARAMETER—A,
                    PARAMETER—B.
                ENTER COBOL.
```

The corresponding statement in the calling module would be

CALL 'SUBMOD' USING FIELD—A, FIELD—B.

where FIELD—A corresponded to PARAMETER—A and FIELD—B corresponded to PARAMETER—B. In other words a reference in 'SUBMOD' to the field NAME would refer to bytes 4—23 of the area FIELD—A in the calling module. If more than one layout is required of a single area then the REDEFINES clause may be used. A name which appears in a linkage section entry may be passed as a parameter to a called module.

BAL/Usercode

Access to remote areas can be done in one of two ways (or a com-bination of both). Once the remote parameter area address has been loaded into a register then fields within that area can be referenced using the basic operand format:

```
        L       6,0(1)
        MVC     4(7,6) = C 'EXAMPLE'
```

The disadvantage of this method is the ease with which mistakes can be made when accessing a large number of fields in one area. The solution is to reference all the fields symbolically for which a USING
80

statement and an area description is required. The remote data area is described in this case by use of the DSECT (dummy section).

```
                              ⋮
                    USING     P1,6
                    USING     P2,7
                    LM        6,7,0(1)
                              ⋮
                    MVC       FLDEX, = C 'EXAMPLE'
                              ⋮
P1                  DSECT
                    DS        F
FLDEX               DS        CL7
COUNT               DS        PL4
P2                  DSECT
NAME                DS        CL20
CODE                DS        XL2
STATUS              DS        XL4
                    CSECT
```

The MVC statement in this example is equivalent to that shown in the previous example. If required, more than one different layout can be given to an area by using multiple DSECT or by restructuring one of them:

```
                    USING     P1,6
                    USING     P3,6
P1                  DSECT
P2                  DSECT
P3                  DSECT
                    CSECT
```

or

```
                    USING     P1,6
D1                  DSECT
                              ⋮
P3                  ORG       P1
                              ⋮
                    CSECT
```

PL/1

Remote area descriptions can, as with all PL/1 data declarations, be expressed explicitly (DECLARE statement) or implicitly (default values). An area is indicated as remote, and therefore as requiring no reserved core storage, by the appearance of its name in parentheses after a PROCEDURE statement.

> SUBMOD: PROCEDURE (P1,P2,P3);
>
>   DECLARE 1 P1,
>
>   2 NAME CHARACTER (20),
>
>   2 CODE DECIMAL FIXED (6,0),
>
>   3 STATUS BIT (8);
>
>   DECLARE P3 CHARACTER (40);

Note that the second parameter P2 is implicitly declared but will still not reserve any storage area because of the appearance of its name after the PROCEDURE statement.

EXTERNAL AREAS

As we have already seen, external areas are available in PL/1 and BAL/Usercode, although their method of use is slightly different. In PL/1 complete areas are communicated between modules whilst in BAL/Usercode only the address of an area is used. Note that in practice complete areas will be communicated in BAL/Usercode by the use of DSECT's.

External Areas in PL/1

An external area is identified in PL/1 by use of the keyword EXTERNAL in a DECLARE statement.

> DECLARE PEXTRN CHARACTER (100) EXTERNAL;

Any other procedure (or module) may reference this area by declaring within itself a definition of PEXTRN with identical attributes. Since the compiler is unable to verify declarations in individually developed modules it is essential to ensure that the correct name and attributes are given to areas to be used externally.

External Areas in BAL/Usercode

A single address is communicated between modules by means of the EXTRN and ENTRY statements. The ENTRY statement informs the

assembler that a name is to be known externally and causes an entry
to be generated in an object table identifying the name and its location
within the module. The entries in this table can be used by the linkage
editor or composer to resolve external references when modules are
linked together. The EXTRN statement correspondingly informs the
linkage editor or composer that a name is external to a module and
requires to be resolved from the table in another module. An alternative
to the EXTRN statement is to pick up an external address by means
of a V-type address constant (*see* Module Base Address, Chapter 12).
In some operating systems the occurrence of an external name in a
module will initiate a search of the system library in an attempt to
find a matching reference. This feature (AUTOLINK) can save the
programmer the trouble of ensuring that all the modules he requires
are available in object deck form in his link edit or compose job
stream. Since only addresses are communicated it is not necessary to
define areas of equal length particularly if only the beginning of an
area is required in a given module.

The use of external areas in BAL/Usercode is illustrated below:

```
MODA        CSECT
            BALR      3, 0
            USING     *, 3

            CALL      MODB

AREA1       DS        CL100
AREA2       DS        CL50
            ENTRY     AREA1
            ENTRY     AREA2

MODB        CSECT
            USING     *,15
            STM       14,12,12(13)
            EXTRN     AREA1
            L         3, = A(AREA1)
            L         4, = V(AREA2)
            USING     3,DS1
            USING     4,DS2

DS1         DSECT
            DS        50CL1
```

```
DS2        DSECT
           DS        CL50
           CSECT
```

SAVE AREAS

When control is returned from a called module to its calling module
the general registers contents must be as they were immediately before
the call was made. In order that this can be done the called module
must save the registers immediately it is entered. However, the called
module cannot establish addressability for its internal storage areas
prior to storing registers since to do so would involve corrupting at
least one register. A register save area must therefore be supplied, in a
free register, by the calling module. By convention register 13, on entry
to a called module, will contain the address of an area in the calling
module where the registers can be stored.

    If the called module is now to become a calling module it must
repoint register 13 to its own internal register save area. However, it

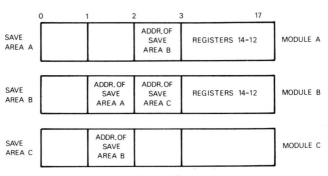

Figure 13.1

must also save the address of its calling modules save area in order
that a correct return can be made. Provision is made to store the calling
modules save area address in the save area of the called module. The
save area also has space to store the address of the save area of the
next lower level module. Thus a module in the middle of a hierarchy
will have a pointer to the previous save area and to the following save
area. Similarly, with the save areas on either side. The save areas are
said to be chained together. Figure 13.1 illustrates this. Each save

84

area consists of 18 words the first of which is not used. Word 1 is used to store the address of the previous save area and word 2 the address of the next save area. Registers 14 through 12 are stored in words 3 through 17. Register 13 itself is not saved with the other general registers.

Coding to accomplish the chaining required for module B above is shown below:

```
          MODB       CSECT
                     USING  *,12
1                    STM    14,12,12(13)
                     LR     12,15
2                    ST     13,SAVE+4
3                    LR     9,13
4                    LA     13,SAVE
5                    ST     13,8(9)
                            :
                            :
6                    L      13,4(13)
7                    LM     14,12,12,(13)
8                    BR     14
          SAVE       DS     9D
                     END
```

The sequence of events in the coding is as follows:

(1)   Calling modules register values saved in calling module's save area (displacement of 3 words from register 13 address).

(2)   Address of calling module's save area saved in this module's save area (chain back link).

(3)   Calling modules save area address temporarily stored.

(4)   Save area register reset to identify save area of currently active module.

(5)   Address of this module's save area stored in save area of calling module (chain forward link).

(6)   Save area register reset to point to calling module's save area.

(7)   Calling modules register values reset.

(8)   Return to calling module.

Fourteen

DATA MANIPULATION

As we have seen in Chapter 13 it is desirable to allocate an individual base register to each parameter area. If this is not the case every reference to a field within a remote area will invoke a considerable amount of address computation and manipulation. (Each time a field is referenced a base register must be initialised.) In order that each area may be given a unique base register it is necessary to limit the number of parameters that can be passed to a module. It is recommended that no more than five data areas be so passed.

There will obviously be occasions when more than five fields are to be communicated to another module. This does not present a problem if it is recognised at the modularisation stage when a large number of non-contiguous items and some small structures can be combined into one or two large structures. This combination can also save core storage since individual items defined at an 01 level will force boundary alignment onto a double word. However, in a structure only the initial entry and half and double-word binary fields require alignment. To avoid this binary field alignment the coding will vary according to the language in use. In Cobol the only solution is to avoid the use of the USAGE COMPUTATIONAL clause although PL/1 provides the UNALIGNED keyword. Programs written in BAL/Usercode can obviously avoid alignment problems by not using the DS F or DS H statements; however, if this is the case then great care must be taken to ensure that no register-to-storage arithmetic is attempted without first aligning the field required:

```
                MVC     FWORD,BINVAL
                A       3,FWORD
                MVC     FWORD(2),BINVAL2
                AH      4,FWORD
BINVAL          DS      CL4
BINVAL2         DS      CL2
FWORD           DS      F
```

86

When data area layouts are being designed some thought should be given to compiler forced alignment that is likely to occur. Each time forced alignment takes place core storage is being wasted and it is often possible to avoid this wastage by restructuring the data layout. Consider these examples:

Cobol

```
01 ACCUMULATORS.
    02 FILLER OCCURS 20.
        03 TOTAL PICTURE 9(6) COMPUTATIONAL.
        03 CODE PICTURE X.
```

BAL/Usercode

```
TOTAL    DS   F
CODE     DS   CL1
ACCUMS   ORG  TOTAL
         DS   20CL8
```

PL/1

```
DECLARE 1 ACCUMULATORS ALIGNED
          2 FILLER (20),
            3 TOTAL BINARY FIXED (6),
            3 CODE CHARACTER (1);
```

Each of these structures has 60 bytes wasted by the full-word alignment requirement of 'TOTAL' since the occurrence of 'CODE' after each full-word will produce three slack-bytes to the next full-word. However, by simply re-structuring the area as shown below the wastage is completely avoided.

Cobol

```
01 ACCUMULATORS.
    02 TOTAL PICTURE 9(6) COMPUTATIONAL
        OCCURS 20.
    02 CODE PICTURE X OCCURS 20.
```

BAL/Usercode

```
ACCUMS   DS   0F
TOTAL    DS   20F
CODE     DS   20CL1
```

PL/1

```
DECLARE 1 ACCUMULATORS ALIGNED,
          2 TOTAL (20) BINARY FIXED (6),
          2 CODE (20) CHARACTER (1);
```

In each case the coding required to access these fields is the same whichever way the areas are structured:

Cobol   IF CODE-IN = CODE (SUB) ADD TOT TO TOTAL (SUB).

```
BAL/Usercode    LOOP    LA      4,8(4)
                        CLC     CODEIN,0(4)     Main loop only
                                                shown
                        BNE     NEXT
                        A       3,0(4)
                        ST      3,0(4)
```

PL/1   IF CODEIN = CODE (SUB) THEN
                         TOTAL(SUB) = TOTAL (SUB) + TOT;

THE ALLOCATION OF STORAGE

The availability and allocation of core storage is a major consideration
in any programming task. Core storage will be required, not only for
the programs processing instructions, but also for I/O areas, work areas,
look-up tables and so on. Storage required for a given module will be
defined either in the module itself or in a data module and will be
allocated when the program commences execution. This effectively
means that all working storage areas are active throughout the execution

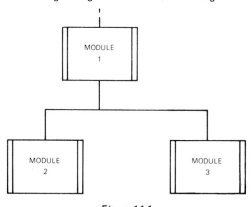

Figure 14.1

of the program although clearly this need not be the case. Suppose, in
the module linkage chart shown in Figure 14.1, that each module
requires 200 bytes of working storage. The total allocated within the
program phase will be 600 although not more than 400 bytes will be
active at any one time. If it were possible to de-allocate core storage
when it became deactivated the overall program requirement would be
88

considerably reduced. (Core storage which has been de-allocated is available for use by another module.) Users of PL/1 can invoke Automatic or Dynamic Storage allocation (DSA) by use of the AUTOMATIC, BASED and CONTROLLED attributes in data declarations. Users of other languages will need to use a simulated DSA technique.

SIMULATION OF DYNAMIC STORAGE ALLOCATION

Let us first of all look at a simple example with only one lower level of modules (Figure 14.2). Suppose the working storage requirements are 300 bytes for module 1 and 400 bytes for each of modules 2, 3 and 4.

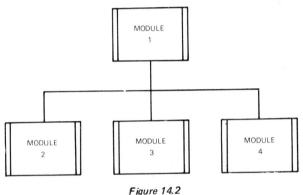

Figure 14.2

If storage was allocated directly for each module the total used would be 1500 bytes although only 700 bytes are active at any time.

Module 1 will be coded with 700 bytes of working storage which will be split into two groups. The first group of 300 bytes will be used by module 1 for its own working storage. The second group of 400 bytes will be passed, by module 1, to each of the other modules in turn for use as their own working storage.

Module 1   WORKING-STORAGE SECTION.
                01   WORK-STACK.
                      02 MODI-AREA   PICTURE X(300).
                      02 STACK-AREA PICTURE X(400)..

             PROCEDURE DIVISION.

89

CALL 'MODULE2' USING STACK-AREA.
CALL 'MODULE3' USING STACK-AREA.
CALL 'MODULE4' USING STACK-AREA.

The lower level modules would be coded in a conventional fashion —
Modules 2, 3, 4   LINKAGE SECTION.
    01   WORK-STACK-AREA.
        02 - - - - - - - - - - - - - - -
        02 - - - - - - - - - - - - - - -
        02 - - - - - - - - - - - - - - -
    PROCEDURE DIVISION.
        ENTRY 'MODULE2' USING WORK-STACK-AREA.

The technique can now be extended to module linkage charts with a
greater depth-level and complexity although the method remains the

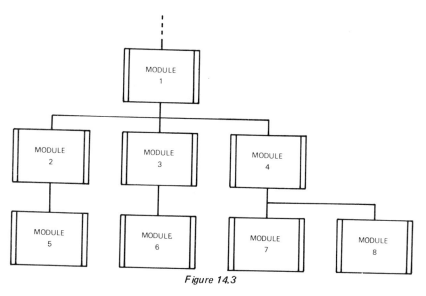

Figure 14.3

same. Consider the module linkage chart shown in Figure 14.3. Suppose
the working-storage requirements for this chart were as follows:

Module 1	200 bytes
Module 2	300 bytes
Module 3	250 bytes
Module 4	275 bytes
Module 5	150 bytes

                    Module 6   140 bytes
                    Module 7   120 bytes
                    Module 8   100 bytes
The total required is therefore 1535 bytes although the maximum that
can ever be active is 650 bytes (module 1, module 2, module 5). When
the storage requirements of each of the modules is different the total
required for the work-stack area is the sum of the largest requirement
at each level. The first level will pass to the second level an area large
enough for the second and third levels. The second level will then pass
to the third level an area for the third level only.

Module 1   WORKING-STORAGE SECTION.
                    01   WORK-STACK-AREA.
                         02 MOD1-AREA   PICTURE X(200).
                         02 STACK-AREA   PICTURE X(450).
                              .
                              .
                              .
                    PROCEDURE DIVISION.
                              .
                              .
                              .
                         CALL 'MODULE2' USING STACK-AREA.

Module 4 (second level)

                    LINKAGE SECTION.
                    01   WORK-STACK-AREA4.
                         02 MOD4-AREA   PICTURE X(300).
                         02 STACK-AREA4 PICTURE X(150).
                    PROCEDURE DIVISION.
                         ENTRY 'MODULE4' USING WORK-STACK-
                           · AREA4
                              .
                              .
                         CALL 'MODULE7' USING STACK-AREA4.
                              .
                              .
                         CALL 'MODULE8' USING STACK-AREA4.

Module 7 (third level)

                    LINKAGE SECTION
                    01   WORK-STACK-AREA7.
                         02 - - - - - - - - - - - - - - - -
                         02 - - - - - - - - - - - - - - - -

PROCEDURE DIVISION.
    ENTRY 'MODULE7' USING WORK-STACK-
        AREA7.
The same technique is used in BAL/Usercode as shown in this example:

MOD1	CSECT	
	:	
STACK	DS	0D
	:	
	DS	~
	:	
STACK2	DS	CL450
	:	
	CALL	MOD2, (STACK2)
	:	
	CALL	MOD3, (STACK2)
MOD2	CSECT	
	:	
	L	2,0(1)
	USING	STACK2,2
	:	
	LA	1,300(2)
	ST	1,STADDR
	LA	1,STADDR
	CALL	MOD4
	:	
STADDR	DS	F
STACK2	DSECT	
	DS	—
	DS	—
STACK4	DS	CL150
	CSECT	
	:	
MOD4	CSECT	
	:	
	L	3,0(1)
	USING	STACK4,3
	:	
STACK4	DSECT	
	:	
	CSECT	

92

Note that in MOD2 the call to next level cannot be made in the normal manner — CALL MOD4, (STACK 4) — the expansion of this call macro would attempt to generate an A-type address constant for STACK4:

```
           CALL MOD4, (STACK4)
     +     L     15, = V(MOD4)
     +     LA    14,*+4+2+1*4
     +     BALR 1,15
     +     DC    A(STACK4)
```

Since STACK4 is defined within a DSECT an attempt to generate this A-type constant would result in an error diagnostic in the assembly listing.

DATA AREA DEFINITIONS

When the data module concept is in use it is necessary to repeat the layout definition of an area in several modules. To recode the layout each time is not only a waste of time but is prone to error. Whilst to duplicate a deck of cards is less error prone it presents maintenance problems (especially if somebody drops the cards!). The ideal solution is to catalogue the area definition onto a system library and retrieve it from there each time an assembly or compilation is required. Some languages (e.g. PL/1) require the use of a pre-processor to do this since they do not have the copy feature, however, the extra time required is far outweighed by the advantages of having to maintain only a single copy of the area definition.

GLOSSARY

ABSOLUTE ADDRESS	An address which indicates the precise storage location of the referenced operand expressed in the actual machine code numbering system.
ACTIVE DATA	Data that is currently in use or has a continuing value.
ASSEMBLER	A computer program that operates on symbolic input data to produce a machine readable output. An assembler will perform such functions as: translation of symbolic operation codes into machine operating instructions, assigning storage locations to instructions, computation of absolute from symbolic addresses. An assembler will normally translate on an item-by-item basis.
BASE ADDRESS	A part of computer storage address which serves as a base, index or starting address for the modification of subsequent addresses.
BRANCH	The unconditional transfer of control from one part of a program to another. Synonymous with jump and transfer.
CALLED MODULE	A module that receives control from another module at an entry point and expects to return control to that module via a return point.
CALLING MODULE	A module that passes control to the entry point of a called module and expects control to be returned (via a return point in the called module) to the statement following the call.
COMPILER	A computer program more powerful than an assembler. In addition to its translating function a compiler is able to replace certain input statements with groups of instructions or sub-routines.
COMPOSER	System/4 version of linkage editor.
CONTROL MODULE	A module that controls the overall logic of a program, by directing the sequence in which

other modules are called. A control module will not normally perform any processing except that needed to determine the above-mentioned sequence.

DATA MODULE — A module containing all the data areas for a program. This module, if present, will do no processing other than to call the control module.

DEPTH LEVEL — A number indicating the number of levels or hierarchies in a module linkage chart.

DUMMY MODULE — An artificial module inserted in an object deck to satisfy a CALL from a module under test. A dummy module consists only of an entry point and a return point.

ENTRY POINT — A point within a piece of coding to which control may be passed by another routine or by the system loader. An entry point name is known to the linkage editor or composer.

EXECUTIVE — Same as supervisor.

FLOATING POINT — A form of number representation in which quantities are represented by a number multiplied by the number base raised to a power, e.g. $384 = 3.84 \times 10^2$ and could be represented as $3.84,2$.

FLOWCHARTING SYMBOLS — The symbols used for flowcharting in this book conform to the USA Standard X 3.5 (revised 1968) and are defined as follows:

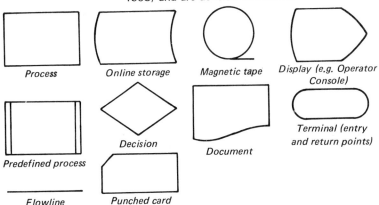

Process

Online storage

Magnetic tape

Display (e.g. Operator Console)

Predefined process

Decision

Document

Terminal (entry and return points)

Flowline

Punched card

I/O MODULE	A module which performs an input/output operation for a single file. The I/O module will automatically open the file when first called.
J.C.L.	Job Control Language — the source statement language used to communicate requests to the supervisor.
LINKAGE EDITOR	A computer program which combines the outputs of language translators (assemblers and compilers) into executable phases. The linkage editor will attempt to resolve all external references in the routines being edited.
LOADER	A part of the supervisor system used to load programs from the system library into core storage prior to execution.
LOOP	A sequence of instructions repeated until a specified condition exists.
MACRO INSTRUCTION	A mnemonic source language statement, used in assembly languages, that produces a variable number of machine instructions.
MODULE	A piece of relocatable coding, having an entry point and a return point, which can exist on its own. A module is assembled or compiled on its own, can be tested on its own and usually performs a single logical function.
MODULAR PROGRAMMING	This is a system of developing programs as a set of interrelated individual units (called Modules) which can later be linked together to form a complete program.
MODULE LINKAGE CHART	A chart showing the hierarchy and relationships of modules within a program.
OBJECT DECK	The machine readable output of a language translator (assembler or compiler).
OPERATING SYSTEM	A collection of computer programs, usually supplied by a computer manufacturer, designed to control and simplify the operating of a computer. An operating system can include a supervisor, housekeeping routines, job scheduler and linkage editor.
OVERLAY	The technique of repeatedly using the same areas of core storage for different stages of a program.

96

	A part of a program no longer required can be replaced, or overlayed, by a new section.
OVERLAY PHASE	A phase that is loaded into core storage during execution of a program and overwrites another overlay phase and/or is overwritten by another overlay phase.
PARAMETER	An area which is passed to a lower level routine or module and whose value can be different at different times during the execution of the program.
PHASE	A module or group of modules that have been processed by the linkage editor to form a loadable and executable routine. Except under special circumstances a phase is not relocatable. A phase will normally reside on a system library.
POINT OF INVOCATION	The point at which control is transferred to a predefined process (thus invoking that process). This point is normally represented by a CALL statement.
PREDEFINED PROCESS	A named process consisting of one or more program steps specified elsewhere, i.e. a subroutine or a module.
PROCESS MODULE	A module which performs a single logical function or a group of small related logical functions. A process module may, as part of its processing, call other process modules or I/0 modules.
RELOCATABILITY	The ability to write a program or module without being aware of the core storage address which the coding will eventually occupy. Relocatability is made possible by the use of the base/displacement mode of addressing (*see* Chapter 13).
RESOLVING	The action of the linkage editor in relating an external name in a module to an entry point, and therefore an actual address, in another module of the same program. Some linkage editors have the ability to search the system libraries in an attempt to resolve external references.

RETURN POINT	The point within a module at which control is returned to the calling module.
ROOT PHASE	A phase which is loaded by the supervisor at the start of program execution and remains in core storage until the program terminates. A program may contain only one root phase.
RUN TIME	The time at which a program is executed as opposed to the time at which it is assembled or compiled. Synonymous with object time.
SPOOL	An acronym for Simultaneous Peripheral Operation On-Line meaning the printing of data from tape or disk in a multi-programming environment.
SUPERVISOR	A permanently resident program designed to control the sequence and loading of production programs, the scheduling of input/output devices and the abnormal termination of programs. Communication with the supervisor is via J.C.L. cards or the operator's control console.

INDEX